OBJECTIVES AND OUTCOMES

Core Concepts in Therapy

Series editor: Michael Jacobs

Over the last ten years a significant shift has taken place in the relations between representatives of different schools of therapy. Instead of the competitive and often hostile reactions we once expected from each other, therapists from different points of the spectrum of approaches are much more interested in where they overlap and where they differ. There is a new sense of openness to cross-orientation learning.

The Core Concepts in Therapy series compares and contrasts the use of similar terms across a range of therapeutic models, and seeks to identify where different terms appear to denote similar concepts. Each book is authored by two therapists, each one from a distinctly different orientation; and where possible each one from a different continent, so that an international dimension becomes a feature of this network of ideas.

Each of these short volumes examines a key concept in psychological therapy, setting out comparative positions in a spirit of free and critical enquiry, but without the need to prove one model superior to another. The books are fully referenced and point beyond themselves to the wider literature on each topic.

Forthcoming and published titles:

OBJECTIVES AND OUTCOMES:

QUESTIONING THE PRACTICE OF THERAPY

Jenifer Elton Wilson
and
Gabrielle Syme

Open University Press

Open University Press
McGraw-Hill Education
McGraw-Hill House
Shoppenhangers Road
Maidenhead
Berkshire
England
SL6 2QL

email: enquiries@openup.co.uk
world wide web: www.openup.co.uk

First published 2006

A catalogue record of this book is available from the British Library

ISBN 10: 0335 210 244 (pb) 0325 210 252 (hb)
13: 9780 335 210 244 (pb) 9780 335 210 251 (hb)

Library of Congress Cataloging-in-Publication Data
CIP data has been applied for

Typeset by BookEns Ltd, Royston, Herts.
Printed in the UK by Bell and Bain Ltd, Glasgow

Dedicated to all users of psychotherapy and counselling and those who try to serve them honestly and usefully.

Contents

List of tables and figures

Tables

Figure

Series editor's preface

A major aspect of intellectual and cultural life in the twentieth century has been the study of psychology – present of course for many centuries in practical form and expression in the wisdom and insight to be found in spirituality, in literature and in the dramatic arts, as well as in arts of healing and guidance, both in the East and West. In parallel with the deepening interest in the inner processes of character and relationships in the novel and theatre in the nineteenth century, psychiatry reformulated its understanding of the human mind, and encouraged, in those brave enough to challenge the myths of mental illness, new methods of exploration of psychological processes.

The twentieth century witnessed, especially in its latter half, an explosion of interest both in theories about personality, psychological development, cognition and behaviour, as well as in the practice of therapy, or perhaps more accurately, the therapies. It also saw, as is not uncommon in any intellectual discipline, battles between theories and therapists of different persuasions, particularly between psychoanalysis and behavioural psychology, and each in turn with humanistic and transpersonal therapies, and also within the major schools themselves. If such arguments are not surprising, and indeed objectively can be seen as healthy – potentially promoting greater precision in research, alternative approaches to apparently intractable problems, and deeper understanding of the wellsprings of human thought, emotion and behaviour – it is nonetheless disturbing that for many decades there was such a degree of sniping and entrenchment of positions from therapists who should have been able to look more closely at their own responses and rivalries. It is as if diplomats had ignored their skills and knowledge and resorted in their dealings with each other to gun slinging.

The psychotherapeutic enterprise has also been an international one. There were a large number of centres of innovation, even at the beginning – Paris, Moscow, Vienna, Berlin, Zurich, London, Boston USA; and soon Edinburgh, Rome, New York, Chicago and California saw the development of different theories and therapeutic practice. Geographical location has added to the richness of the discipline, particularly identifying cultural and social differences, and widening the psychological debate to include, at least in some instances, sociological and political dimensions.

The question has to be asked, given the separate developments due to location, research interests, personal differences, and splits between and within traditions, whether what has sometimes been called 'psycho-babble' is indeed a welter of different languages describing the same phenomena through the particular jargon and theorizing of the various psychotherapeutic schools? Or are there genuine differences, which may lead sometimes to the conclusion that one school has got it right, while another has therefore got it wrong; or that there are 'horses for courses'; or, according to the Dodo principle, that 'all shall have prizes'?

The latter part of the twentieth century saw some rapprochement between the different approaches to the theory and practice of psychotherapy (and counselling), often due to the external pressures towards organizing the profession responsibly and to the high standards demanded of it by health care, by the public and by the state. It is out of this budding rapprochement that there came the motivation for this series, in which a number of key concepts that lie at the heart of the psychotherapies can be compared and contrasted across the board. Some of the terms used in different traditions may prove to represent identical concepts; others may look similar, but in fact highlight quite different emphases, which may or may not prove useful to those who practice from a different perspective; other terms, apparently identical, may prove to mean something completely different in two or more schools of psychotherapy.

In order to carry out this project it seemed essential that as many of the psychotherapeutic traditions as possible should be represented in the authorship of the series; and to promote both this, and the spirit of dialogue between traditions, it seemed also desirable that there should be two authors for each book, each one representing, where practicable, different orientations. It is important that the series should be truly international in its approach and therefore in its authorship; and that miracle of late twentieth-century technology, the Internet, proved to be a productive means of finding authors, as well as a remarkably efficient method of communicating, in the cases of some pairs of authors, half-way across the world.

This series therefore represents, in a new millennium, an extremely exciting development, one which as series editor I have found more and more enthralling as I have eavesdropped on the drafts shuttling back and forth between authors. Here, for the first time, the reader will find all the major concepts of all the principal schools of psychotherapy and counselling (and not a few minor ones) drawn together so that they may be compared, contrasted, and (it is my hope) above all used – used for the ongoing debate between orientations, but more importantly still, used for the benefit of clients and patients who are not at all interested in partisan positions, but in what works, or in what throws light upon their search for healing and understanding.

Michael Jacobs

Acknowledgements

The concept of this series of books and the titles were Michael Jacobs', as was the idea that we might enjoy writing together. Indeed he was right and we have both enjoyed the challenge and fun of writing together. We are grateful to him for all of this and his acceptance of our long time scale. We have also appreciated his input into the text with helpful additions and amendments.

We want to thank all our psychotherapy and counselling friends and colleagues and our clients because it is from them we have learnt so much. However, any errors are not their responsibility but ours.

We also want to thank our husbands for their support and forbearance in a process that has involved hours of absence, both in body and mind! An added bonus has been meeting each other's husbands and planning future work-free fun.

CHAPTER 1

Objectives of this book

Introduction

In this introductory chapter, we intend to open up some of the questions that become prominent as we think about the *objectives* and *outcomes* of psychological therapy. It seems appropriate to broaden and to define this particular terminology. An *objective* could also be called a purpose, an aim or a goal, dependent on the intentions, aspirations and motivation of the person concerned. Immediately this raises the question of whether there is some significant difference between the objectives held by the individuals offering psychotherapy and the people using their services. An *outcome*, in this context, takes place as a result of engagement in therapy and could be construed as positive or negative by either participant. Outcomes are usually linked with ideas of effectiveness and practitioner competence, as indicated by whether change is considered to have occurred. Ideally, outcomes would be demonstrated by some sort of description or measurement, which brings in the difficult question as to whose conclusions are valid, those of the client, the practitioner or a third party, perhaps a researcher. This, of course, depends on the criteria followed regarding the desired outcome, which returns us smartly to the question of motivation as expressed as an objective at the beginning, or birth, of the therapeutic endeavour. And if that was the birth, is the outcome indicative of some sort of death of a living process? All these definitions are inevitably influenced by the social and cultural context of the therapy. Our own intention, or objective, is to use this chapter to hold a dialogue about some of these ideas on a personal level and then to explore the specific issues arising in the subsequent chapters.

We both see ourselves as practitioners of psychotherapy *and* of counselling and are unwilling to differentiate clearly between these two activities. While accepting that psychotherapists, as named professionals, often claim to work at a deeper level on lifelong problems and issues, our experience is that clients who present for counselling also bring longstanding problems, rooted in their childhood experience, and that most counsellors are equipped to work with these issues. Conversely, the description of therapeutic counselling as shorter term work, focused on current problems, is one that could be applied to behaviour therapy and to cognitive therapy, both of which have professional bodies which are situated within the United Kingdom Council for Psychotherapy (UKCP) and firmly claim to be models of psychotherapy, not counselling. To some extent, humanistic schools of psychotherapy, such as gestalt therapy and person centred therapy, also tend to concentrate on the here and now of the therapeutic relationship. Some practitioners, although qualified as psychotherapists, choose to be called counsellors to avoid any suggestion that they are part of the medical profession. They are antithetic to many aspects of a medical approach to illness, such as diagnosis, labelling and a paternalistic approach to patients. In fairness to the medical profession many medical practitioners do not behave in this manner.

Training courses maintain the difference between counselling training and psychotherapy training for several reasons, some of them are historical and others seem to be based on a hierarchical structure. The latter sees the progression from counsellor to psychotherapist as linear. Hence a counselling training is a preliminary to a more advanced psychotherapy training. Another route to becoming a psychotherapist is through a psychology masters degree or doctorate that leads to a qualification to work as an applied practitioner, either as a clinical or as a counselling psychologist. Probably the greatest difference between all these labels or qualifications is in the context of employment and remuneration. In general counsellors are paid less than psychotherapists and clinical psychologists. The majority of counsellors work in independent practice but they often supplement this with posts in agencies, primary care, organizations and further and higher education. Psychotherapists usually work in independent practice with some input to the health service and to university counselling services. Clinical psychologists are trained within the National Health Service (NHS) in the UK and go on to work, almost exclusively, within that organization. Counselling psychologists, trained in higher education settings under the auspices of the British Psychological Society (BPS), work in almost all the settings listed above but are, at the time of writing, still not accorded equal pay or status in the NHS. All these practitioners would see themselves as working psychotherapeutically and as therapists working with those who are mentally distressed.

For the British public, counselling has been seen as a more accessible and normalizing form of help than psychotherapy, which, when it is not confused with psychiatry, is often linked closely to psychoanalysis, considered to be the most exclusive, and costly, form of psychological therapy. This book is written for *all practitioners of psychological therapy*, whatever their affiliation or categorization. Wherever possible we will refer to practitioners and to their practice, but we see the words counselling and psychotherapy as interchangeable and will often use the word *therapy* to cover both activities. It is possible, of course, that this book may interest some users of psychological therapy who are interested to know what motivates people to use therapy and what happens anyway. We welcome this interest.

Aims of the book

The initial question for us is our own objectives and outcomes in writing this book. If we did not know whom it is for and why we are writing it there would be no sense in writing anything. In the same way psychotherapists and counsellors need to know why they are doing what they are doing. We all had personal objectives that drew us to train as therapists; the outcome was becoming professionally qualified. We then have personal aims or objectives in working and continuing to work as therapists and presumably, unless we are masochists, we have an idea of outcomes we hope for and feel a sense of achievement when we see these desired results. Likewise our clients have objectives that led them to seek therapy and experience an outcome when the therapeutic relationship ends. Whether the outcome is in line with their objectives is one of the many interesting questions we will explore in Chapter 6.

This book is therefore for: anyone working as a therapist who is asking, 'Why am I doing this?'; anyone who is concerned about whether they are making any difference to their clients' lives and whether clients really meet their objectives; anyone who wonders if they could make a better initial assessment; those questioning whether being a therapist is a worthwhile occupation; those wanting to understand why some therapeutic relationships work well and others fail; those who wonder whether their own explanations for failure or success are really valid or simply self-justification; and those who question whether change ever happens. These questions overlap so much in this chapter we have split them into six core questions which we address briefly.

Our method throughout this book is to discuss together whatever issues arise from the area being addressed by sharing and exploring our different viewpoints and experiences rather than by arguing about them. In this first chapter, we take each of the above questions in turn and subject them to an initial analysis, each commenting on the other's individual thoughts and understandings. In Chapter 2, we carry out an overview of the main theoretical orientations, each of us contributing our specific knowledge of any one orientation and its particular approach to the objectives and outcomes of psychotherapeutic engagement. In Chapter 3, Gabrielle initiates a consideration of the contexts in which therapy takes place and their influence upon both the aims and hoped for results of clients and practitioners. Chapter 4 reviews the relevant research which has taken place and which continues to examine issues of psychotherapy process and outcome. Jenifer initiates this chapter with a particular focus on how practitioners can use this body of work and can themselves develop a more research minded attitude to their practice, and Gabrielle provides a commentary. In Chapter 5, Jenifer leads a discussion about how assessment sessions may influence outcomes. In Chapter 6, we reflect upon how specific types of outcomes do, or do not, link up to original objectives. This takes us into a joint reflection upon the future, of both the subject of this book and this profession – is it indeed an 'impossible enterprise'?

We include a fair amount of references to relevant literature, but above all we want this book to encourage readers to explore the issues of psychotherapeutic objectives and outcomes, motivations and results, in more detail and depth for themselves and through their own experiences. So we have tried to limit ourselves to key texts, those that have informed our own thinking, and we have appended a Further reading section to the end of the book.

Introduction to the authors

Although we have challenged each other throughout the process, in personal discussions we have been astonished at our likenesses in terms of life experiences. For instance we went to different schools but the hypercritical head of the senior school for one became the headmistress for the other. We both experienced not being part of this woman's 'in-crowd'. As therapists we have both been influenced by a combination of the existential humanistic approach of Rogers and Yalom, and of psychodynamic theory, with a focus on the insights of object relations (Winnicott, Bowlby and Guntrip in Buckley 1986). We both work in a nurturing rather than deprivatory style. We have both been heavily involved in student counselling (Elton Wilson 1994) and currently work in independent practice (Syme 1994). But there are differences: Jenifer describes herself as an integrative therapist whereas Gabrielle practises in an integrative way, simply because that is the product of long experience rather than a specific theoretical approach. Gabrielle does predominantly long-term work whereas Jenifer has specialist knowledge of brief work (Elton Wilson 1996). Jenifer on occasion deliberately uses a cognitive behavioural approach whereas Gabrielle does not. While we have both worked within the NHS, Gabrielle as a child psychotherapist and Jenifer as a counselling psychologist, for Gabrielle it was largely a negative experience whereas for Jenifer it was inspiring. The reasons for the difference and for Gabrielle's negative experience were mainly to do with complex institutional dynamics rather than the children and their families, who were a fascinating group with whom to work. For Jenifer the experience was so good because she was trusted to work with a very challenging client group, without having to manage complex institutional problems.

It is these similarities and differences that inform all our interactions in this chapter and those that follow.

Our preliminary questions

What is my objective/aim in working as a therapist?

Gabrielle
There are both conscious and unconscious reasons for working as a therapist. What arises from self-knowledge for one person might be an unconscious responsiveness to human need for another, so I am not going to separate the reasons into these two categories but simply to discuss the varied motivations and objectives which result in someone training as a psychotherapist and then practising as one.

A number of people choose to study counselling, psychotherapy or psychology in a search to understand themselves and others. Some of this group do not go on to be therapists, having discovered what they needed to know and not wanting or needing to be involved in the journey of self-discovery of others. Graduates of courses who do go on to practise have a variety of motivations. One is a genuine concern, empathy and interest in other people and pleasure in seeing someone's inner turmoil and pain reduce. However, there are many other motives that need to be considered to prevent an inappropriate use of one's clients.

It is commonly said that all therapists are simply wounded healers seeking their own healing through being therapists (Jung [1954] 1966): their unconscious objective is to offer the healing to others that they need for themselves, thus having a vicarious experience of healing rather than an actual one. I believe this can be true, but that a good enough training will draw this to the attention of trainees so that, once acknowledged and attended to by having a necessary period of therapy themselves, therapists are then less likely to damage their clients through this need being unrecognized.

For some there is an idealistic objective that the world would be a better place if people were more self-aware and so, for example, offered less damaging parenting to their children. Their hope is that by being therapists themselves they will be part of a force which will eventually be of sufficient size to cause a major societal shift. Closely allied with this objective is the one of doing 'good'. A do-gooder can be a very controlling and tricky person to manage because much of what they do is driven by their own needs rather than those of the person they are 'helping'. They feel better by 'doing good' to a person they have identified as being in need of help. As a young widow I often fell victim to the do-gooders who felt sorry for me and saw various solutions to my problems but did not help me discover my own solutions. A number of people who become therapists have a need to be loved, and certainly at some stages in the therapeutic relationship one can expect to be idealized and feel 'beloved'; but in a complete therapy this is only a phase and arises from the transferential relationship. There are also likely to be stages of anger and hate, based on past non-functional relationships, before a final resolution where the therapist is accepted for what he or she is: a person with all the foibles and faults that make one human. If the desire to be loved is a powerful objective then the necessity to be firm and confrontative on occasions may be very difficult and so the outcome of the therapy can be unsatisfactory.

I initially decided to train as a therapist having been a member of an analytic group. On one occasion I was talking with some despair of my 10 year old son's rebellious behaviour. The analyst's response was, 'Haven't you done a good job!' This unexpected, and to me paradoxical, response helped me realize that there was a quite different way of thinking about people which was non-judgemental and had as its aim an understanding of why people did things outside of their own awareness. After my very prescriptive parenting this was a release and I became determined to learn more and to endeavour to approach people from this viewpoint.

The outcome of seeking training is to gain knowledge, skills, attitudes and insights that enable the therapist to sustain relationships with troubled and mentally ill people. The therapist then has objectives when working with clients and their desired outcomes, and this subject will be a major part of other chapters in this book. However, there are occasions when working therapists also ask themselves, 'Why am I doing this?' Perhaps any practising therapist should ask themselves this regularly, because all emotionally draining work can cause burnout in the practitioner with a resulting loss of interest in the client's needs. Questioning oneself and searching for an answer often does result in a recommitment to the therapeutic endeavour. If the answer to the question is, 'I don't know why I am doing this', 'I'm tired of looking after others' or 'I would rather be doing something else' then this needs action. It would be important to take this conclusion to a supervision meeting, to discuss whether only a holiday was necessary or whether in fact one should no longer be doing the job. It is essential to the therapeutic relationship that both the therapist and client are committed to the endeavour.

Jenifer
My response to Gabrielle's discussion of the motivations and objectives that lead people to train as psychotherapists or counsellors is initially one of full agreement. I particularly endorse the motivation to understand others and that of the wounded healer, although I am less sure that personal therapy does always enable the healer to bracket off his or her own pull towards a vicarious healing experience. However, when I turn to my own experience, and that of some of my supervisees and trainees, I want to underline and intensify the search for self and for other understanding with a more youthful motive, one of intense curiosity about how other people behave in the way they do. It was this that drew me to graduate in psychology, traditionally the study of human behaviour, before specializing in a variety of forms of psychological therapy. This burning curiosity is not, in my case, and in the case of many of my supervisees and trainees, purely intellectual. It can be an essential strategy for survival learnt in childhood.

In my case, I was sent to school in England at the age of 7 years and did not see my parents, or speak to them, for four years. It was essential for me to study other people, especially strangers, very carefully to find out how to be accepted by them. Of course, this also led to my concealing my own needs in an attempt to accommodate the preferences of other people. All of which resulted, after years of dissembling and with the help of my own psychotherapy, in me finally becoming curious about myself, who I really was, what I really felt and needed. Curiosity about, or interest in, other people can lead an individual into psychotherapy training and then reveal depths of unacknow-ledged fear and pain. This can then show the way to a more profound curiosity about other people's hidden depths, their 'real selves' (Masterson 1985).

As for the therapist's own need to be loved by their clients, clearly this can lead to a misuse of the therapeutic relationship to meet the practitioner's own needs. Again, insight into this motivation, and an ability to contain it, is the answer for those who persist as practitioners, as Gabrielle points out. I think here of the reported remarks of Rogers with respect to his own motivation to become a therapist. He is said to have realized that his own loneliness arose from a lack of social skill. Presumably, he is a good example of somebody who contained and then sublimated this desire into the development of a theoretical and practical approach based on social awareness and ability.

As for the regular recurrence of this question of motive, my view is that although, as Gabrielle warns, repetitive and weary self-enquiry as to the purpose of our work as therapists can indicate burn out, at another level it can inspire a genuine enquiry into our practice as working therapists. In particular, my own interest in the outcomes of therapy has been sharpened by periods of internal questioning on whether my clients benefit from my interventions and from my offer to accompany them on their voyages of self-discovery. That is why I use, and recommend to others, regular informal reviews with clients of their progress, and why I have become involved in the development of a user-friendly doctoral programme for therapists. Perhaps the question could now move on from my own motivation to be a therapist to the nature of my role in respect of my clients' progress from *objective* to *outcome*.

Am I making any difference to my clients' lives?

Jenifer
Almost all clients come into therapy with life problems, even if these are sometimes hidden behind abstract or vague feelings of discomfort, or are not clearly obvious in their everyday lives. These problems are usually manifested overtly in the client's social interactions, causing distress and discomfort to them and to those around them. More rarely clients bring their own inner feelings of dissatisfaction with their lives, lives which to others seem to be functional and even successful. In either case, this may be a temporary state of disturbance or a recurring chronic condition. The general objective, stated or otherwise, for almost all clients, is to change their life experience, at least to some extent, and to live in a more contented, harmonious way. Sometimes they express a wish to understand themselves better and this aim is usually a more achievable aim from the practitioner's point of view.

It is here that an uncomfortable question arises for many of us as practitioners. Is insight enough, even when accompanied by greater emotional clarity and a new way of observing our interactions with other people outside of the consulting room? It is generally agreed that major learning for the client takes place through the therapeutic relationship, whether that be in the form of a 'corrective emotional experience' (Alexander and French 1946) or by means of a 'Socratic' debate to counter negative and irrational thinking (Beck et al. 1990; Ellis 1994). To change at all clients seem to need to trust their therapist's professional knowledge and personal good will. Thoughts and emotions are influenced in the room, but what happens in the client's external world? Psychotherapy depends on a belief that its effectiveness is demonstrated in this capacity of the client to put into practice these different ways of thinking, feeling and relating in their lives. To encourage this to happen cognitive and behavioural models of practice build in 'homework' in the form of behavioural experiments to be carried out at home. Other modalities such as gestalt and transactional analysis recommend a focus on experimental changes made in the consulting room and through the therapeutic relationship. Psychodynamic therapists rely on the subtle changes which take place through the emotional intensity of the transference which may then transform other meaningful relationships in the outside world.

There exists for many thoughtful practitioners an uncomfortable level of uncertainty as to how much of the precious self-understanding gained through therapy is used by their clients to actually improve their life conditions. At the same time most practitioners hold as a main tenet of their professional activity that changes in cognition and affect, which take place in the therapeutic context, must always have some effect on a client's general functioning. This is sometimes referred to as a change of *attitude*, defined as a system of core beliefs maintained by emotional experiences, which thus shape behaviour. Another way of putting this is that many clients experience, through a consistent, truthful and empathic relationship with their therapist, a new understanding of their potential interactions with the outside world, and are emboldened to act differently in that context. Against this stands the uncomfortable evidence from the now mainly forgotten body of psychological research into attitude change, (Hovland and Rosenberg 1960) which demonstrated the lack of congruency between revised attitudes as verbally stated, and any observable change in behaviour. What Frank and Frank

(1991: 30–4) describe as the client's 'assumptive world' is indeed difficult to shift without the energy which comes from emotionally grounded insight and a real wish for change.

Gabrielle
I have little to add to what Jenifer has written. As she states, thoughtful practitioners always wonder how far self-knowledge is transformed into changed lives. Balanced against this are the many testimonies therapists have from their ex-clients. I have some contact with a number who finished therapy over 10 years ago. They tell me that the self-knowledge acquired during therapy has resulted in them feeling more confident, accepting and loving themselves more, being able to make a long-term committed relationship, being more secure, less judgemental, being able to leave a destructive marriage, recovering from the death of a loved person and so on. They are also telling me of sustained differences. But of course that is only a few and they may be telling me what I want to hear. I do not hear from many others, either perhaps because therapy made no difference to their lives, or because it made their lives worse or because they have no desire or need to keep in touch with me, or to tell me that therapy made a difference to their lives.

Many therapists have another reason to believe that therapy changes lives and that is their own experience of therapy, for this experience is often a prerequisite of training courses and has been a prerequisite for accreditation as a counsellor with BACP. It is perhaps this experience that convinces practitioners that therapy has an effect. In my own case I had had a catastrophic life event which had left me disillusioned and depressed. I appeared to others to manage life well but in fact I lacked confidence and was very defensive over many issues. By the end of therapy I was ready to make a new long-term relationship, had stopped biting my nails, believed in myself and was more tolerant of myself and others. Thus there were behavioural and emotional changes. However, I do not think I have changed in my core; I have become better able to manage life and relationships on a day to day basis. I also know that in a crisis and when stressed I can again doubt myself, believe that nobody loves me and so on. This leaves a question for me about what people mean by 'making a difference' in their lives. In my case I believe therapy has made a long-term difference despite the absence of the change in certain stressful situations.

Another source of information on whether therapy has made a difference to clients' lives are partners, families and close friends. Upon enquiring from my partner whether he thought therapy had made a difference to me, he was sure that it had helped in managing the stresses of a reconstituted family, but he did not think I had changed dramatically. All this may confirm is that the core of a person does not change, even if they manage themselves and life better.

Of course change in a person is not always acceptable to their partner. If the outcome of therapy is that the client can leave a marriage, this may not be what their partner wants. Some years ago a well known writer, Fay Weldon, wrote with considerable anger about the effect of therapy on her partner. Another group of people who accuse therapists of damaging clients are parents who believe that therapists have planted false memories and turned their adult children against them. In both these instances the aggrieved parties are testifying to changes having occurred as a result of therapy. So the change is not seen as good by all the parties.

Clearly it is very difficult to really ascertain whether therapy has made a difference to a client's life because the client's experience and the observed changes may well not match. This is a challenge to the researcher and also to the practitioner when assessing the client's objectives.

Do clients meet their own objectives?

Gabrielle
A therapist's task is to help clients meet their objectives and thus this frequently asked question is important to all therapists. The reasons clients give for seeking psychotherapy (and therefore their objectives) are very varied. Sometimes they are very concrete, centred around an event or a phase in their lives such as a death, a miscarriage, having relationship difficulties, a breakdown of a relationship or redundancy; but their reasons are just as frequently rather more abstract. Examples might be that they are generally not happy; they have low self-esteem and lack confidence; they have lost their way; they want to be married; they are lonely and cannot make friends; they do not know who they are; they do not like themselves, their self-image or their appearance; they are unsure of their sexual orientation, or they

feel an outsider and in some way different from others. For some their loneliness, lack of fulfilment, lack of self-confidence, etc., renders them so dysfunctional that they become depressed, suffer from acute or chronic anxiety, or act out through obsessional behaviour, eating disorders, addictions or self-harm. This group may seek medical help and are then referred to psychotherapists and counsellors, but they may equally self-refer.

In the case of some of the concrete examples, relatively short-term work focused on the problem in their life is often all that is wanted and needed. Thus the client's objective, to work through bereavement or redundancy, is clear and their objective is met. However, it is often not as straightforward as this. In some instances the reason stated by the client turns out to be a way of gaining entry to wider help, and perhaps a way of discovering whether they are taken seriously, whether they feel safe with the therapist and whether they can talk. Then the objective may change.

For some time Jim had been wondering whether there was someone to whom he could talk about his lack of girlfriends. A friend had talked about having been to the counselling service. Jim began to think about whether he could talk to counsellors, but he feared that they would think he was weird. He plucked up courage and went to the counselling service. When the counsellor, Mike, asked what had brought him, he replied that he was having difficulty in studying and was worried because exams were only a few weeks away. Mike elicited quite a lot of information from Jim, but felt there was something else troubling him. He wondered out loud about this. Jim felt enormous relief at this and then started, albeit tentatively, to talk about his lack of girlfriends and how he wondered if he was gay; and how he felt different from other students.

In this scenario the client rapidly reveals that there is a much more important objective that he really wants to attend to. Client and counsellor can then identify a new objective to which they are both committed. However, it can be much longer before the real objective is revealed and so become the new focus of the work. The late revelation may be because the client feels so shamed by their problem. This could, for example, be in the area of sexual fetishes, perhaps because society at large is so judgemental about sexual differences. (I have deliberately used the words *sexual differences* rather than *perversions* because the latter word has so many punitive connotations, and to illustrate how terminology can make it difficult for many people to reveal their preferences, in this case sexual.)

Objectives can change for other reasons. Often as therapy proceeds, and the client gains in confidence and self-knowledge, a client's objective such as, 'I want to form a long-term relationship with someone', might change into, 'I want to like myself and become my own friend, content with my company'. This could happen in the case of Jim in the above extract. Sometimes this change in objective happens because clients begin to understand their needs in a different way. A client may realize that unless they like themselves and their own company they are unlikely to form a fulfilling relationship with someone else. On other occasions the therapist and client review where they have got to and specifically look at whether the initial objectives have developed or changed.

There are many reasons why the client's *objectives* are not always met in the *outcome*. Sometimes failure happens because the therapist mistimes an intervention or frightens the client so much that they leave – prematurely in the therapist's view, wisely in the client's! But failure may not be because of poor practice. Events in a client's life after therapy has begun may so disrupt them that the therapy becomes untenable. Some clients become so stuck in their patterns of behaviour that their objective is unachievable. This may be due to poor technique on the part of the therapist, but it may also indicate a genuine impasse for the client. Perhaps the client is not prepared enough to meet the objective – though there is a danger that this conclusion reached by a therapist may be seen as patronizing and self-justificatory. Nevertheless it is also possible to suggest (though not necessarily to the client) without being judgemental that there might be a 'secondary gain' for the client in the old behaviour, making change difficult to follow through.

Part of the object of assessment is for therapists to discover the client's objective and then to decide whether they can work with a client to achieve this objective. Sometimes the honest answer from the therapist is that the client's objectives are unrealistic. A more realistic objective may then be found by talking over the issues and reframing them. The danger in doing this is that the client may agree because they want therapy and not actually because they want to embrace the new objective. On other occasions the therapist knows that they do not have the skills or necessary empathy to work with the client's objective. For instance, I am not empathic to alcoholics, having been very frightened and abused as a child by a relative who was an alcoholic. I therefore know that I cannot create the necessary environment to help an alcoholic and it would be unethical to agree to work with one.

When thinking with clients about their objectives and one's task as a therapist in helping them meet their objectives, it is important to remember that all clients have their own cultural context. This particularly needs to be recognized if there is dissonance between the therapist's and the client's context. Cultural differences can be ethnic but they are as likely to be political, social, spiritual or religious. A client might be very right wing politically and the therapist left wing. If the therapist has a covert objective to make the client more liberal, along with the overt objective, stated and agreed with the client, this is unethical and will disrupt the therapy. Indeed the client may not meet their objective.

In thinking about whether clients meet their own objectives and why they have not done so, it is important to get a balance between self-questioning, a function of the internal supervisor (Casement 1985), realism and a kindness to oneself, for even the best of therapists will not succeed with every client. We are after all only human!

Jenifer
Reading Gabrielle's thoughts about whether clients really met their objectives, I was once again struck by how much a client's stated objectives are linked to their level of motivation at the time that they come for therapy. My experience is that initial objectives, or goals, as expressed by most clients tend to be vague and global – to feel better; to be as competent or as happy, as they used to be; to be heard. Where the problems and the objectives are more concrete, indeed, as Gabrielle suggests, 'relatively short-term work focused on the problem' is probably going to be sufficient. Nevertheless, I would argue that in many current contexts time for therapy, whatever the nature of the problem, *is* limited, either by the service provider or by the client's own choice. In such cases, in my experience, the

practitioner can always aim to facilitate the beginning of a process of psychological change. At the very least, the client can learn that talking to another person can be useful and may seek out professional help at another time. Such practice encourages a practitioner to stand down from their responsibility to *do the whole job* and to accept that clients will continue on their journey of personal development in their own time and in other contexts.

I was struck by Gabrielle's very correct guidance as to the practitioner's need to withdraw when they recognize their own lack of empathy or skills with regard to a specific client's stated objectives. Sadly, some practitioners have little opportunity to choose their clients or to refer them to others, and are faced with a demand to see all clients sent to them in the context in which they work. If this is the case then supervision becomes particularly important.

A more worrying issue is the presence of a clash of objectives between client and practitioner based on different belief systems and different cultural contexts. Early in my work as a clinical supervisor, I had a supervisee who held strong, warm and passionate feminist beliefs. Her initial session with an Asian woman, who was seeking to be a better wife to her husband, led the therapist to work hard to raise her new client's consciousness of her rights as a modern woman. Supervision led her to understand the danger of this approach, and to ask herself whose aims she was imposing. Too late, she heard that her client had been beaten by her husband and would not be returning to the counselling agency.

Gabrielle discusses objectives that are not met and suggests that this could be due to poor practice or to the client's life situation becoming untenable. The re-negotiation of goals by means of a series of intermediate and collaborative reviews is, for me, a central part of my own practice. Most usually the objective becomes more realistic and achievable, although I have also found that there is often a move towards a search for psychological change in attitude and in emotional response, rather than the initially stated concrete goal of, for example, finding a better job, finding an intimate relationship or divorcing a life partner. This increased insight is rewarding but usually needs to be accompanied by some form of changed behaviour so that the client can return to their outside life with new energy and appetite.

At this juncture, I seem to be arguing for the probability of some sort of difference being made by psychotherapy practitioners to their clients' lives, even though the type of change will differ according to the motivation of the client. It is my deep conviction at this stage of my own development as a practitioner, that the match between client motivation and practitioner commitment is vital to any reasonably satisfactory outcome of psychotherapy. That this motivation relies on trust in the practitioner as a warm, non-judgemental and honest person, who possesses a valid enough explanation for the client's distress, is another story.

Is being a therapist a worthwhile occupation?

Jenifer
This question is one that could easily be answered, from a purely subjective view, with a big, 'Yes'. I spend hours and days listening to people telling their stories, and doing my best to understand and to convey an understanding of their pain and distress. I offer myself as a trustworthy person free from any personal involvement with their life concerns and willing to offer my full attention. As I listen, I am using my experience of interpersonal dynamics and child development as a backdrop to each story. I am taking in the non-verbal messages just as much as the words being spoken and am looking out for any dissonances and contradictions. I am alert for indications of patterns of relationship and repetitive survival strategies. Even with new clients, if I remain intensely attentive I might be able, tentatively, to offer some useful response which sheds a different light on the events and feelings recounted. Often this response is grounded purely in the present moment, and refers to the present situation. At other times what is going on in the room can be shown to be linked to what happened in the past, as well as what is happening in the client's present life. If nothing changes, then the future may also be a repetition, unless we can together explore alternative ways in which the client can face their present situation.

All this seems to be a useful contribution to the life of another person, and is based on years of professional training and clinical experience. But is it all an elaborate social game? Am I really in the business of using my own assumptions to influence and adjust another person's mode of existence? Alternatively, am I focusing too much on the past, on the causes for the client's present distress, when what is needed is a focus on solutions, on changed behaviour, on reassurance? Perhaps the client would do as well, or even better, if they talked things through with a friend, a member of their family or any unqualified but reasonably sympathetic person. Often clients start out with a simple wish to talk and to be heard. Other clients ask for advice and an externally administered cure or solution. I offer them the more complex route to change through self-understanding, basing my approach on the books I have found inspiring, the teachers I have observed and my own experience of working on myself. Maybe I do this because I need to affirm and justify the effort and financial resources put into my own training experiences, which led to the professional qualifications I now hold. I see my work partly as a search to uncover and clarify my clients' underlying and possibly outdated beliefs about their social worlds – but perhaps I need also to question my own professional belief system. The challenge offered by this book is to provide an opportunity to consider various points of view and to test assumptions we hold dear to us.

One point of view would be that, as practitioners, we can only view our work as worthwhile if there is some valid external evidence to support our way of working with clients, and to show that it leads, in most cases, to a satisfactory outcome. For this we would need, at the very least, to ask our clients about their levels of satisfaction from our work. There is a risk that they will tell us only what they think we want to hear, so strong is the need to please. Those who are dissatisfied are more likely to express their dissatisfaction to an external person although, with enough trust in the relationship, some clients do risk expressing negative feelings directly to their therapists. Perhaps we should also try to find a way to check out whether there has been any observable change outside the consulting room in the client's own social world. Here the difficulty is that of breaching the confidentiality usually promised as a standard condition of any engagement in counselling or psychotherapy. All this points towards the importance of practitioners beginning to consider how they might evaluate their work, a subject explored in greater depth in Chapter 4.

Gabrielle
For me the answer is also a resounding, 'Yes!' I enjoy my job because I like being with people and find them endlessly

fascinating. No two people are the same, even if in an initial assessment I might identify a pattern of behaviour I have come across before, or if I am working with a common presenting issue such as bereavement. I am never bored. But enjoying the job does not of itself mean the work is worthwhile. It is worthwhile because I feel rewarded when I know I have been part of a process that has made a difference in people's lives. I see people blossom, find themselves, able to make new relationships, recovering from depression or lack of confidence or the blow of bereavement, and reinvesting in their lives. Finding a job worthwhile is a privilege but it carries with it responsibilities. I have a duty to check that my assessment of client's needs and objectives is accurate and not driven by my own needs. I also must ensure that I am not seeking a successful outcome just to satisfy my need to make a difference and be worthwhile. It is not whether I feel worthwhile but whether the client really has benefited from therapy. Regular supervision helps me to monitor this but there is a need for research to monitor whether therapists' belief that there has been a successful outcome is borne out by clients.

Why do some therapeutic relationships work well and others fail?

Gabrielle
There is no doubt that some therapeutic relationships work much better than others and that some do actually fail. This is as true within an individual's therapeutic practice as it is that some therapists are better than others. I know that I have done much more sensitive and enabling work with some clients than with others, and that I have also failed with some. Occasionally I see a potential client who arrives with considerable caution because a previous therapeutic relationship has not worked even though there has been no malpractice.

There are factors both in the therapist and the client that contribute to a therapeutic relationship that works. It is important that the client and therapist both want to work together and that they have an agreed objective, timescale and outcome at the start of the therapeutic relationship, even if these later change. There are some commonly agreed principles of ethical practice. Therapists must assess whether they have the skills, knowledge and experience to work with a particular client so that their objectives can be achieved. It is also important to look at one's client load and the needs of existing clients. It is essential to limit the number of clients one takes on and also ensure that the needs of the clients vary. For instance, it is difficult to sustain more than two highly dependent clients at any one time. The client should ideally be well motivated and not coming simply to please someone else. However, it is quite common for clients only to become really motivated as they feel safer with the therapist and realize that they can get something from therapy.

All the essentials mentioned can be in place yet some relationships will be much more successful than others and some will still fail. The most successful therapeutic relationships are those where the therapist is able to really understand the client and form a working partnership in which both client and therapist have a common aim. They also have to be well attuned to one another, just as the good enough parent is, with the therapist able to attune to most of the changing needs of the client (Stern 1985; Winnicott [1954] 1992). It is much easier to be intuitive with some people than others, and this may be because of marked similarities between the therapist's and the client's life experiences. However, these similarities can also result in a poor alliance because the therapist cannot separate their experiences from the client's. It may be easier to hear some clients than others, because they are more able to project their feelings; some may be more difficult to work with because they are ambivalent about changing their lives. Even with a good empathic ability it can be a long time before the therapist hears the message. One reason is that if the therapist is blind to issues in himself or herself then they cannot be seen in or heard from anyone else. This is one reason given for therapists having therapy themselves. I myself noticed that, after therapy, suddenly I was hearing the issue of envy being mentioned by a lot of my clients. I wondered how long it was that I had been deaf to the topic of envy. It is a testament to the patience of clients and the strength of the therapeutic relationship that they have stayed and eventually enabled me to hear them. Another reason for not hearing an issue is lack of experience in the therapist. I have on occasion agreed with a client that we have gone as far as we can go together and therefore ended the therapeutic relationship, but they have subsequently returned and then worked at a much deeper level. In this instance there were probably two factors at work. One was that I was considerably more experienced on the second occasion and therefore probably a 'safer' person. The second factor was that the client had consolidated the previous work and possibly was stronger, or in a better place personally to do work which might prove more disturbing than anything we had undertaken earlier.

Overall, there needs to be more than good assessment and accurate ascertainment of objectives for a relationship to work well and even when both of these are in place a therapeutic relationship can fail. Is there some feeling, almost body chemistry, which also has to match for a therapeutic relationship to work well? This could just be seen as a way of making therapy mysterious and inaccessible to research but it does link with the idea that there are some therapist qualities and probably some client qualities necessary for a therapeutic relationship to work well and for the client's desired outcome to be reached.

Jenifer
I find this last paragraph of Gabrielle's both thought provoking and stimulating. For me the most overlooked aspect of the therapeutic relationship is this mysterious question of match between the participants, and its influence on both objective and outcome. There has been some research into the importance of matching therapist to client (Frank and Frank 1991) but this has tended to be at the pragmatic level of age, gender, class and cultural background. All these are important parameters and, in particular, ethnic similarities and differences have been much agonized over. It is, however, the more subtle elements of a shared journey undertaken by 'fellow travellers' who are 'joined together in facing the questions that have no answers' (Yalom 2001: 8–10) that fascinate me as I engage with a client. Why is it that I personally often feel more attuned with and attracted to the struggles of clients who seem to be at the cliff edge of their lives, angrily challenging the therapeutic environment, rather than to earnest trainee therapist clients who are willing to adapt and conform. I struggle with dependency as a characteristic in a client and yet can empathize with a fiercely held and destructive counter-dependency, which was originally developed as a strategy for survival against feelings of abandonment. These preferences are partly explained by a perceived similarity to my own strategies for survival, but there is something more. The deepest attunement that I can achieve with a client is present

when I detect that we are, ultimately, both searchers, questioning the more socially acceptable human aim to reduce suffering and to increase contentment, Freud's 'pleasure principle' ([1920] 1984). This realization leads to what has become for me a burning question. What is the interface between the goals of psychological therapy and the purposes of this search for meaning and inner transformation? This question underlies much of my contribution to this book.

Gabrielle mentions the need for some clients to close down their therapeutic journey and then to return later to work at a deeper, more advanced level. She suggests that this could be because the client had consolidated previous work and was in a stronger place in themselves, and/or that the therapist was more available to work with previously defended against issues. For many years now, I have been refining a stage model of the client's journey through personal development over time, usually using a series of therapeutic encounters, not necessarily with the same therapist (Elton Wilson 1996: 29–47). So far, I have seen the therapist's role to discern and to work with the stage being presented by the client, and to accept that other practitioners may have already facilitated the earlier stages, or may become those who will work with later stages. It is an added richness of concept to take into account the personal development stage of the therapist as a factor in a client's journey. In any case, this way of approaching psychotherapeutic work with a client encourages practitioners to let go of the somewhat grandiose belief that they are responsible for the client's whole psychotherapeutic engagement. A stage model of this kind can also be a useful tool in assessing with a client what work is needed now, as well as being an encouragement to review together whether enough has been accomplished at this time in the client's own evolving process of development and change.

How valid is the therapist's explanation for failure or success?

Jenifer
This question also asks if such an explanation could in some cases be simply a self-justification? In addition, it is important to me to remember that a therapist's views regarding the failure or success of any therapeutic enterprise must be based on their own current worldview, their cultural conditioning and their notions

about the overall purposes of psychological therapy. As human beings we all tend to defend fiercely these fundamental belief systems, and as therapists we have usually extended and elaborated our values through the training we have undertaken. Almost all these trainings emphasize the importance of the therapeutic relationship and are likely to list the therapist qualities needed to maintain this professional commitment as a positive influence upon a successful outcome. To admit failure of the therapeutic encounter can be seen by the practitioner as an admission of failure as a human being. The temptation to find a suitable, and soothing, self-justification is great.

Early research, particularly that carried out within the psychoanalytic orientation, tended to rely upon the practitioner's views of success or failure. More recently, attempts have been made to obtain a wider picture by asking clients themselves, and even asking for external evidence from family members, friends and work colleagues. For myself, I remain interested, above all, in my clients' views regarding the ongoing process, as well as the outcome and how these views change over time. These views are rarely expressed in terms of success or failure, but more subtly attend to relative levels of emotional release, personal self-affirmation or small but significant changes in problematic relationships. Of course, these more tentative judgements may be influenced by my client's wish to please or challenge me. Confidentiality agreements restrict me from asking others in my client's external world, although occasionally enlightening reports of comments or complaints from these others enter the consulting room. To submit my practice to the scrutiny of an external evaluation instrument, or to an outside researcher, has been a useful and challenging source of information. However, I notice my reluctance to use routinely any form of standardized evaluation in my ongoing practice. Maybe there is a particular danger to the experienced therapist in asking himself or herself to engage with clearly framed questions about the success or failure of their own therapeutic engagements. In Chapter 4, I note the apparent reluctance of many qualified practitioners to engage with issues of outcome or even objective.

Part of the problem with assessing the success or failure of a therapeutic engagement is that so often the client's original reason for entering therapy has been left behind or superseded. While this may be a result of the client deepening their own understanding of what is needed, I think that as practitioners we need to consider how much we are influencing these changes of direction through our own subjective views about the good life and our own belief systems about the purposes of psychotherapy. We may be alert to the restrictive assumptions held by our clients, but less so to our own assumptive worlds. Do we betray our clients by quietly sidelining their original aims and goals, and encouraging them to engage in the level of personal exploration that we ourselves needed to undertake in order to become therapists? Increasingly, as I move toward the final stages of our contemplation of the disturbing questions listed at the beginning of this chapter, I realize how much we may all need to question our hidden attitudes to objectives and outcomes. How much can we take on board Ann France's definition (1988: 243), from a client's point of view, of psychotherapy as 'a co-operative venture between two equals, with the same goal of effectively enhancing the life of the consulter, and freeing him or her from the temporary bond created with the therapist'?

Gabrielle
I agree with all Jenifer has said. This is by far the most difficult question to face because I want my chosen profession and my way of working to help the client and therefore to be successful. I must therefore always be on the lookout for my desire to see the therapy as successful. I found challenging Jenifer's remarks about the power of my world view arising from my cultural conditioning and also wonder how far I subtly, and not so subtly, influence and change my client's objectives. I suspect that I do.

Supervision is very important because it is here that I routinely look at my work and my explanations and understanding of why some interactions are more effective than others. As each therapeutic relationship ends I challenge myself, as does my supervisor, on whether the relationship has been successful. We ask whether the client has completed the work and reached their objectives and if not why not. If I assess a relationship as having been a failure it is because I do not believe that there have been changes in their approach to life or in their attitude(s) to themselves. On occasions I have viewed a relationship which has ended very abruptly as a failure, but this has not been the view of my supervisor. Some clients need to finish abruptly and perhaps my desire for a 'proper ending' comes from my mind-set and world view that 'good endings' are very important. It may be very important for me but for some people there is a need to get on with life, to slough off the dependency and to go. I have to respect a client's right to leave in the way they wish, and I need to judge failure by a more objective measure than my subjective ideas. What I illustrate here is that the judgement of success or failure is likely to be subjective. What is important, and the raison d'être for this book, is for therapists to think more objectively about how to measure success and failure, how to improve the client's experience and how to be confident rather than defensive about the merits of their psychotherapeutic interventions.

CHAPTER 2

Overview of the main orientations

Introduction

The objectives and outcomes of psychotherapy, both for client and for practitioner, are likely to be heavily influenced in their formulation by the main theoretical orientation under which the psychotherapeutic interaction takes place. This may seem surprising when generally a client would take the same problems and distresses to any therapist, without any consideration of the therapist's theoretical orientation. Usually clients are concerned to find somebody whom they can trust to help them, and their focus at the first meeting is likely to be on the personality and the professionalism of the therapist. However, this chapter surveys the main theoretical orientations for the following reasons.

First, in spite of a slow but probably inevitable move towards an integrated approach to psychotherapy practice, emphasizing the 'common factors' influencing effectiveness across all approaches (Grencavage and Norcross 1990; Wampold 2001), most practitioners still align themselves with a particular 'school' of therapy. As a result, the handling by practitioners from different orientations of the first or early sessions in which objectives are ascertained can be very different. There is considerable disagreement among practitioners from the different orientations, and also within orientations, about assessment and diagnosis or formulation, which for some orientations would be part of reaching an understanding of the client and how their objectives might be achieved, but for others would be viewed as unacceptable practice.

Second, it seems to us important that clients are given the knowledge of what to expect and why therapists approach understanding the clients' objectives quite differently. For example, some practitioners will, as a matter of principle, use a questionnaire to help identify a client's objectives while others will not.

Third, there is some evidence that certain theoretical approaches are more effective than others in treating specified mental health disorders. For instance, current research suggests that cognitive behavioural therapy (CBT) may be more effective in treating phobias, compulsions, delusions and hallucinations than other forms of psychotherapy (Tantam 1995). This means that if clients present with an objective of managing these particular mental health problems, the therapist, if they are not CBT trained, would be well advised to consider referring them to a CBT therapist.

In 1994 Syme found that in the BAC Counselling and Psychotherapy Resources Directory published the previous year, 143 different theoretical approaches were mentioned. Grencavage and Norcross (1990) reviewed surveys and found that between 1959 and 1986 the number of distinct approaches to counselling and psychotherapy had risen from 36 to over 400. Poznanski and McLennon (1997, cited in Horton 2000) found it hard to objectify different theoretical orientations and have suggested that this is because all have at least four positions embedded in any stated theoretical position, which makes the analysis extremely complex. These are:

- personal therapeutic belief systems which are not always clearly articulated or accessible;
- theoretical school affiliation or the practitioner's self-reported adherence to one (or more) theoretical schools;
- espoused theory or the theoretical concepts and techniques that practitioners say they use;
- theory-in-action or what observers believe the practitioner is actually doing.

In general there is a much stronger link between theoretical school affiliation and espoused theory than between espoused theory and theory-in-action. However, it is not uncommon to find there is no correlation between theory-in-action and espoused theory or what the practitioner says is being done.

Horton (2000) suggests that there are four main elements of a model:

- basic assumptions or philosophy;
- formal theory of human personality and development;
- clinical theory which defines the goals, principles and processes of change and provides a cognitive map which gives a sense of direction and purpose;
- the related therapeutic operations, or skills and techniques.

From the point of view of objectives and outcomes the first two elements will be heavily influenced by the therapist's personal values and beliefs about people, and about sociocultural factors, which in turn are likely to influence how the objectives of a client are both ascertained and articulated. Clinical theories will also have an impact on the naming of objectives by a therapist and the process that the therapist and client follow to bring about change in order to reach a satisfactory outcome that meets the client's objectives. Some approaches, such as psychodynamic counselling or psychotherapy, focus on the origins of a psychological problem and in some instances will diagnose or formulate a psychological problem. Other theories, such as person centred counselling or psychotherapy, focus on the facilitation of the client's self-actualization and do not use the word 'assessment' to describe the first session, neither do they name a psychological problem or diagnose. On the other hand cognitive-behavioural theory would direct the therapist to diagnose a problem and use psycho-educational programmes in order to fulfil the theoretical purpose of the therapy, which is to bring about change.

There have been many attempts to reduce the complexity of the many theoretical orientations by grouping similar approaches together. In this book we have chosen four groupings: psychodynamic, existential-humanistic, cognitive-behavioural and integrative.

Psychodynamic approaches

The aim of the work of the psychoanalyst is to help the suffering patient understand himself (sic) and achieve self-knowledge, particularly of his previously denied and split-off aspects.

(Harold Stewart 1997: 1)

The psychodynamic approaches are all based on the theory and practice of psychoanalysis and are further influenced by the four major theoretical movements, Freudian, Adlerian, Jungian and Kleinian, which grew out of the original theory. Psychoanalysis was developed by Freud as an approach to help mentally disturbed patients at the end of the nineteenth century. From soon after its inception there was schism in the psychoanalytic movement with major disagreements between Freud and his followers. This resulted in people such as Adler and Jung breaking away, in 1911 and 1914 respectively, and developing their own theories of personality development and techniques to help people with psychological problems. With each schism and with each development there was a subtle, and at times not so subtle, shift of emphasis and value. These shifts inevitably affected the attitude towards objectives and outcomes held in each new theoretical outlook. In Britain, alongside the development of Freudian and Jungian 'schools' of psychoanalysis, Melanie Klein was developing her own theories of personality development based on her work with children, which were viewed as sufficiently different from Freud's by the members of the British Psychoanalytic Society that they became known as belonging to the British School as opposed to the Viennese School, brought to London by Freud and applied to children by his daughter, Anna. Nowadays psychoanalytic theory is much more diverse and has been developed by such people as Winnicott, Fairbairn, Guntrip, Bion, Bowlby, Kohut and Fordham.

The theory of modern day psychodynamic counselling or psychotherapy is rarely based on purely Freudian, Jungian, Adlerian or Kleinian theories but is more like an independent school without allegiance to any one school, drawing on ideas from all the psychoanalytic schools, including those mentioned above. Most psychodynamic training courses include all the major schools of thought mentioned, plus the more recent developments. However, in teaching the skills and techniques of working, the fundamental propositions of Freud are made central in all these courses because, despite the different psychoanalytic theories of Freud, Adler, Jung, Klein and subsequent theorists, Freud was the originator of psychoanalytic theory. His fundamental propositions are summarized by Cooper (2002):

- no part of mental life or the way we behave is accidental. It is always the outcome of antecedent conditions;
- mental activity and behaviour is purposeful and goal directed;
- unconscious determinants mould and affect the way we perceive ourselves and others. These are thoughts of a primitive nature, shaped by impulses and feelings within the individual, of which they are unaware;
- early childhood experiences are overwhelmingly important and pre-eminent over later experience.

These fundamental propositions lead all psychodynamic practitioners to believe that personality change takes place for clients throughout their lives, regardless of whether they have psychotherapy or counselling. The objectives of the therapeutic endeavour are to help people become more aware of the themselves, to be able to talk about themselves, to understand themselves better, to acquire insight and thus to become more whole. The task of the therapist is to enlarge clients' awareness of their inner world and how they relate to their outer world. This is done by 'removing amnesias' or 'making the unconscious conscious' through enabling clients to understand how their early infant and childhood experiences were construed and are still played out unconsciously (Freudian); by acknowledging the constant struggle between love and hate (Kleinian); by recognizing how their private logic and mistaken goals are played out in their life style (Adlerian); by fostering individuation or attaining wholeness (Jungian). Through this process, mental activity and behaviour can become purposeful and goal directed in a more fully conscious state thus fulfilling, as a desirable outcome, the Freudian reality principle of 'where Id was, there let Ego be' (Freud [1933] 1973).

A more interpersonal goal has been introduced by object-relations theorists such as Winnicott, Guntrip, Kohut and Bowlby. They have all seen the very early relationships as being key to later psychological health. This has been supported by recent research in the neurosciences, which has used MRI scans and analysis of hormone levels, particularly the corticosteroids, to show that the development of higher brain function is in response to social experiences (Schore 1994, 2001; Gerhardt 2004). These areas of the brain do not automatically develop, they need interaction, both touch and visual, with other people for this to occur. It is from this interaction that the social self develops first, and then gradually the sense of self. Just as important is that this interaction, resulting in the fully developed social brain (orbitofrontal cortex), takes several years to complete and needs verbal and non-verbal input. The verbal input is essential for developing the ability to express and manage feelings. This research has verified attachment theory, originally developed by Bowlby using infant observation and ethology, which focuses on the quality of the early relationships with the significant caregivers (usually, but not exclusively, the parents).

The implications of these discoveries for the therapist are that many clients have not had sufficient social interaction in their early years; as a result parts of their social brain is immature. This makes it difficult for them to interact with others and they autoregulate themselves rather than regulate themselves with reference to others. Research has shown that some parts of the orbitofrontal cortex have recuperative powers. Therefore a major objective of therapy could be to reactivate the client's capacity to be with someone else emotionally, which is largely achieved through the non-verbal relationship. The material outcome of therapy is that the therapeutic relationship has stimulated the maturing of the social brain.

The more systemic therapies, developed within the psycho-analytic framework to address the needs of family therapy and organizational input, are necessarily focused upon a less individualistic outcome. They have been formed in order to improve the quality of mental and emotional health within a community setting, whatever the size of that communal group. The initial objective is very often to improve communication and cooperation, with an ultimate goal of increased understanding of the unconsciously held belief systems holding sway within the family or work group. More realistic decisions can then be made about whether to retain these beliefs or not.

The assessment interviews, which are discussed in a later chapter, are a critical part of practice for a psychodynamic therapist, because they are used to clarify the client's objectives in seeking therapy and to make as informed a decision as is possible on the likelihood of reaching a satisfactory outcome using the therapist's knowledge and skills. The formulation, whether it is in the formal language of a therapeutic model or in a more descriptive language, gives a focus to the work but is not rigid and is open to revision whenever necessary. One of the functions of supervision is to revisit the formulation regularly to check the therapist's understanding of the client and that the client's objectives and needs are being heard and addressed. Whatever the formulation, the objectives and outcomes of this therapy are likely to be focused upon the problems as experienced internally by the client, the original causes of these problems in the client's early experience and the resolution of these problems through insight, emotional catharsis and reality testing. These rather general objectives can result in a lack of focus and the therapy becoming interminable. The emphasis on the past, and on problematic issues, may mean that both the present, in the form of current strengths, and the future, in the form of positive goals and optimistically framed outcomes, are likely to be under-emphasized. There is also a danger that excessive introspection and increased insight do not result in changed behaviour but rather to a justification for behaviour.

Existential-humanistic approaches

The role of therapy is to help people acknowledge and face old hurts, instead of hiding from them; find adaptive ways of dealing with their pain; and explore and express their real self. In short, the therapist helps the client to learn to delight in themselves.

(Elinor Greenberg (1998: 1))

Within this grouping, seven major schools of therapy are usually cited under the following names: existential, gestalt, narrative, person or client centred, primal, psychosynthesis and transactional analysis (Feltham and Horton 2000). Although most of these approaches developed separately, from existential psychotherapy and psychosynthesis in the early part of the twentieth century, to gestalt and person centred therapy in the 1950s, to primal therapy and transactional analysis in the 1960s, and up to the most recent adaptations proposed by narrative therapy, they were all, in part, formed in reaction to the precepts and practice of the psychoanalysis as generated by Freudian theory. Therefore, these approaches are all in part informed by psychodynamic principles, which have either been adapted, replaced or refocused.

The earliest theoretical schools to develop in reaction to

psychoanalytic theories and practices were existential therapy and psychosynthesis. Existential psychotherapy arose from the European philosophical teachings of Kierkegaard, Heidegger and Sartre, with their emphasis on the phenomenological experience of life as central to human well-being. This form of therapy is practised in many different ways with rather different focuses through which to achieve the objective of authentic living. Thus Yalom (1980) talks of the courage to face the givens of human life including death, loneliness, impermanence and the lack of any externally provided meaning: whereas van Deurzen (2002) encourages the exploration of the four dimensions of worldly being: physical, personal, social and spiritual. Jung's theoretical position was also influential in the European development of existential-humanistic theory, as was Reich's emphasis on the role of the body in psychological distress and potential cure (1942, 1949). Reich, like Jung, broke away from Freud's inner circle and his objectives were incorporated in Arthur Janov's primal therapy developed in the 1960s, which describes the need for clients to find and release the 'primal scream' held in their bodies in order to achieve an ideal outcome of relaxed authenticity (Janov 1970).

Psychosynthesis was first developed by Roberto Assagioli, an Italian and a student of Freud. While originally influenced by Freudian theory, the lack of focus on 'creativity, inspiration, spirituality, understanding and higher values such as love, compassion, joy and wisdom' (Whitmore 2000: 358) and lack of recognition of existential questions about the meaning and purpose of life, led him to develop a more Jungian and holistic theory of human development. The objective of the therapy is to facilitate the meeting of the client with their personal and spiritual identity, leading to the desired outcome of an inner freedom resulting in a development of the will and an expansion of awareness and therefore of choices.

The conceptual framework of transactional analysis, developed by Eric Berne and his associates in North America, was, to a large extent, a reaction to psychoanalytic therapy but was heavily influenced by the Freudian structural explanation of personality formation, while adding the pragmatic objective of behavioural change through analysis of the deep structures of social transactions. The id, ego and super-ego of Freudian theory is replaced with the more easy to understand model of Parent, Adult and Child ego states, all of which are potentially available to awareness and not buried in the unconscious. The outcome to be sought is usually formulated as the client's achievement of an 'integrated adult' position, which can consciously make use of the beneficial aspects of both Child and Parent ego states. Through this process clients can follow their own 'arrow of aspiration', which Berne held to be integral to every human being, towards a life based on successful human relationships.

Gestalt theory and practice was developed by Fritz and Laura Perls (Perls et al. 1951). The word 'gestalt' does not have a direct translation into English but close definitions are pattern, configuration, form and whole (Ellis and Leary-Joyce 2000). Gestalt therapy retains the psychoanalytic emphasis on causes arising from the past but emphasizes as an objective the existential responsibility of the individual to let go of his or her false and defensive manoeuvres and live an authentic life in social relationship with others. The task of the therapist is to increase awareness of internal experience and of these patterns of interaction, reveal their origins and encourage real life, here and now experiments towards a more genuine existence. This is both the objective and desired outcome of this type of therapy, and has inspired countless encounter groups and encouraged a highly active, directive form of therapeutic practice.

Narrative therapy focuses on the centrality of story telling in human communication and in making sense of events. Families, communities and cultures all shape our stories as do narrative templates derived from myths, films and novels. Some cultures have a dominant template, which effectively silences a personal lifestory. Inevitably stories are told to one or more people and are co-constructed in dialogue. Depending on the situation the story would be told differently, told in many voices (such as the voice of the parent, the voice of the psychiatrist, the voice of an official, the voice of the child and so on) and told in different styles (habitual stories, personal stories, reports). The tasks of therapy are to ensure the story is told fully and heard; silencing or minimizing of lifestories is damaging and problems are 'understood as being those areas of human experience around which a person is not able, or willing, to engage in conversation' (McLeod 2000: 345). Change comes about with the retelling of the story and the generation of different versions. Thus the objectives of narrative therapy are to assist clients to tell different, satisfying, accurate and more coherent stories of themselves in order to find their true selves.

All the schools that we have mentioned have been hugely influenced by person centred therapy as formulated by Rogers (1967). Using his own experience and supported by carefully conducted research, he made the conditions pertaining in the relationship between client and therapist central to the therapeutic endeavour. These conditions of learning are stated by Rogers as:

- The client feels incongruent and is facing a problem
- The therapist is in a state of congruence with the client
- The therapist provides accurate empathic understanding
- The therapist provides unconditional positive regard
- Communication takes place between client and therapist of these conditions

(Rogers 1967: 281–4)

Person centred theory believes that a client provided with these growth permissive conditions will be able to replace the self-image, imposed upon them by their previous life experience and by society, with a more authentic real self. Central to this process are the non-verbal, here and now forms of communication that are key to the establishment of a truly therapeutic relationship. This is an exact parallel with the understanding of the objectives of therapy arising from Schore's work (1994, 2001) mentioned earlier. The person centred therapist's ability to empathically respect their clients unconditionally and yet remain fully congruent is made central and facilitates this objective. The emphasis is on the present rather than on explanations based on early childhood. The therapist's role as the provider of insightful interpretations leading to emotional catharsis is peripheral to their ability to listen accurately and reflect their client's experience actively. The values and principles behind this theoretical approach have implications both for the objectives agreed with clients and the outcomes aspired to by both therapist and client.

What all existential humanistic approaches have in common is this Rogerian idea of self-actualization, which is the tendency of all human beings to strive for the fulfilment of their potential and the belief that for all people the purpose of their life is a journey towards wholeness. The task of the therapist is to create a nurturing environment of unconditional acceptance, empathy and genuineness or congruence and to introduce himself or herself, as a new person, into the inner world of the client. From this the client is able to face their fear, confusion and anxiety, which will have brought them to seek help in the first place, and challenge their own self-concepts.

The objective of therapy is described by Thorne (2002), who is a person centred therapist, as becoming a 'fully functioning person who is the embodiment of psychological health' and whose primary characteristics are an 'openness to experience, an ability to live fully, and an organismic functioning' (an ability to let what feels right, physically and emotionally, be a trustworthy guide to behaviour). It is unlikely that any person has ever fully achieved this and therefore this ideal can only be a theoretical objective or outcome of therapy. Research by Tausch and Lietaer (cited in Thorne 2002) and Thorne's own observations show that as a result of therapy clients change in their perception of themselves, moving

- away from facades and the constant preoccupation with keeping up appearances;
- away from 'oughts' and an internalized sense of duty springing from externally imposed obligations;
- away from living up to the expectations of others;
- towards valuing the honesty and 'realness' in oneself and others;
- towards valuing the capacity to direct one's own life;
- towards accepting and valuing one's self and one's feelings whether they are positive or negative;
- towards a greater respect and understanding of others;
- towards a cherishing of close relationships and a longing for more intimacy;
- towards a valuing of all forms of experience and a willingness to risk being open to all inner and outer experiences however uncongenial or unexpected.

(Frick 1971, cited in Thorne 2002)

Any one of these ten developments could be an objective or an outcome of Rogerian person centred humanistic therapy, both for the client and the therapist, though clients' objectives are rarely expressed in this way. They are more likely to be focused upon the difficulties they are experiencing in their outside life. There is a danger that the developments listed by Frick (1971, cited in Thorne 2002) for person centred therapy could, paradoxically, lead to clients being sheltered from the realization that the problems that brought them to therapy are often part and parcel of life and it is necessary to take responsibility for their attitude to these problems.

For more existentially orientated theorists, including gestalt therapists, these more realistic and challenging aspects are emphasized and the objectives are more likely to be phrased in terms of honest self-knowledge, courageous confrontation of the trials of human existence and a search for the meaning behind lived experience. The danger here is that the result can be the adoption of a self-absorbed attitude of entitlement, which excludes awareness of the needs of other people. Other more transpersonal theorists, including psychosynthesis practitioners, would support all of these objectives under the over-arching aim of growth of spiritual understanding. Transactional analysts promote behavioural change as a part of self-actualization thus avoiding too loosely defined aims and objectives. However, this bias can veer towards a form of social control based in the current moralities of the dominant cultural environment.

Overall the existential-humanistic therapies are often seen as more positive about human beings' capacity for good than are the psychodynamic approaches. They are criticized for their under-emphasis of human beings' capacity for causing enormous pain and committing heinous acts. The outcomes of these approaches can be that very harmful behaviour towards others and extreme selfishness can be justified on the grounds of self-expression.

Cognitive-behavioural approaches

> The main idea is that if you see things differently then you will feel better.
>
> (Gillian Butler 1999: 1)

> The strategies described in this book can also help you solve relationship problems, handle stress better, improve your self-esteem, become less fearful and more confident.
>
> (Dennis Greenberger and Christine Padesky 1995: 1)

Current applications of the cognitive-behavioural approach to therapeutic practice have developed out of the basic concepts of behaviour therapy as formulated by Wolpe (1982) and others, under the influence of the experimental observations of Pavlov and Skinner. The focus of this early and, at that time, somewhat radical, approach to therapy was to examine problematic behaviours, their origins in learnt responses and the conditions under which these responses were activated. Having made a clear analysis of these behaviours and how they were being maintained, the therapist's objective was to encourage the client to extinguish these maladaptive learnt responses. This was done by changing external conditions through the application of carefully designed interventions, which acted as either positive or negative behavioural reinforcements and resulted in the replacement of the problematic behaviours with more appropriate learnt responses. Thus the primary objective of this early form of psychological therapy was to change observable behaviours rather than to examine the cognitions underlying the behaviours. As behaviour changed, so would the problem manifested in personal experience and social life be resolved.

However, behaviour therapists observed at a relatively early stage that behavioural change depended both on the client's cognitive understanding of the process and on the level of trust that existed in the therapeutic relationship. The belief system of the client seemed to be an essential component in the process of change. Hence cognitive therapy, as developed by Beck (1976) and his colleagues requires therapists to focus initially upon helping their clients to understand the automatic, and usually negative thinking which underlies their unsuccessful responses to life events. Once this objective is achieved, clients are encouraged to monitor their thinking and their behaviour, to 'see things differently' and to move towards an outcome that entails a more realistic and positive approach to their lives. To enable this outcome, it became clear that it was necessary for clients and therapists to form an emotional bond, fostered by sufficient understanding and warmth displayed by the therapists to encourage trust in the clients. This enables them to overcome their fears and take part in active changes of their behaviour.

Ellis (1962, 1994) included more explicitly the emotional aspect of cognition in this process of behavioural change in the theoretical explanations underlying rational emotive therapy (RET). The core concept of this theory is that human beings are dogged by a basically irrational form of thinking leading to self-damaging and inappropriate feelings and resulting in dysfunctional behaviours. With regard to human relationships, this leads the individual to adopt impossible aims and objectives. Typical of these is the belief that one should be liked by every person one meets. When such an irrational belief is not validated, a negative internal self-image is invoked resulting in emotional distress and further problematic interactions, which are then brought to therapy. The task of the therapist is actively to challenge these beliefs, through vivid and lively disputation with their clients, using invented terms such as 'musturbatory thinking' (Ellis 1987: 114) to challenge the fixed patterns of thinking. The immediate objective is for clients to attain a more realistic and rational view of their lives, to feel their emotional life differently and to be able to try out different and potentially more successful behaviours. The ideal outcome would be for clients to move towards 'a more vibrant existence' (Ellis 1987: 108) by achieving some of the following somewhat exacting goals:

● Self-interest
● Social interest
● Self-direction
● Tolerance
● Acceptance of ambiguity and uncertainty
● Flexibility
● Scientific thinking
● Commitment
● Risk-taking
● Self-acceptance
● Long-range hedonism
● Non-perfectionism and non-utopianism
● Self-responsibility for emotional disturbance

(Ellis 1987: 108–10)

Notwithstanding these aspirations, RET therapists hold that almost all human beings are naturally and inevitably wedded to their irrational emotional disturbances and self-defeating behaviours and resist any radical change in this basic human condition.

This rather conservative view of the possible rewards of a cognitive focus in psychotherapy is not overtly shared by the large group of therapists working under the influence of Beck (1972, 1976). The approach of this highly influential school of cognitive behavioural therapy has been firmly focused upon the goal of alleviation of dysfunctional symptoms especially with regard to depression, anxiety, phobias and obsessive-compulsive disorder. The therapy is active, structured, usually short-term and is well suited to established research procedures, such as random control trials (RCTs) which can be used to validate its effectiveness. This has encouraged its popularity in medical settings and, in some ways it has become the therapy of choice in these contexts. More recently, a wider range of emotional disturbances and relational issues has been addressed by Beck's (1985) cognitive behavioural therapy (CBT). The theory proposed is that dysfunctional and abnormal behaviour and emotions are caused by the underlying beliefs, attitudes and assumptions of the disturbed individual.

The task of the CBT therapist is to use a combination of verbal and behavioural techniques to help the client recognize the way they are structuring their reality and to correct and to move to a more realistic view of the situations in which they find themselves. Interventions include 'Socratic' dialogue, questionnaires, diagrams, journals and other forms of 'homework' and the immediate objective is to involve the client in a process of active cognitive change and behavioural experimentation. Inevitably, this means the fostering of a reasonably warm, cooperative working alliance between therapist and client, although the analysis of this relationship is rarely included as part of this strategy. The focus of the therapy has tended to be upon the present situation and the problem presented in therapy. The formation of long-lasting maladaptive cognitive schemas based on early traumatic experience has, over time, become a more central focus of attention by some cognitive therapists (Young and Swift 1988), particularly in the treatment of clients diagnosed with personality disorders. In America, dialectical behaviour therapy (Linehan 1995) has been influential in encouraging a broad range of interventions in this field. The initial objectives of this form of therapy include increased mindfulness, social skills and insight regarding 'invalidating environments' (Linehan 1995: 3) as experienced in their childhoods by clients diagnosed with borderline personality disorder. In addition, the therapy is designed to help clients achieve emotional regulation through the experience of a warm therapeutic relationship.

Cognitive therapies are well suited to a mind-set which views psychological distress as arising from a dysfunction in the way individuals construct their environments. Philosophically, some cognitive therapies have been heavily influenced by a constructivist view of human nature, which maintains that reality is always subjective and that events are dependent on the current social influence experienced by the individual. Fixed theories of cause and of change, such as those proposed by learning theory and those of Freudian psychoanalysis, do not suit this outlook and therapists of a constructivist turn of mind are likely to look beyond the immediate symptom presented. Kelly's ([1955] 1991) philosophy of 'constructive alternativism' proposes that alternative realities were always available and that every person can be understood as if they were scientists, taking part in an active process of construing meaning, making mini-theories out of past experience, forming hypotheses based on their anticipation of what might happen and then taking action. Personal construct therapy was specifically designed by Kelly to encourage clients to examine their own ways of constructing their worlds, emotionally and cognitively, and then carrying out their own behavioural experiments to confirm or disconfirm these personal constructs. The task of the personal construct therapist is to use a series of imaginative and creative techniques to help clients let go of their stuck and habitual patterns and to actively construe the alternatives available to them. The desired outcome is that clients move on, participating more fully in their life choices.

The emphasis on 'mindfulness' as an aid to therapeutic progress, particularly for clients diagnosed as suffering from borderline personality disorder (Linehan 1995), has been an interesting development within CBT. Behaviour therapists have, from the beginning, offered to teach methods of relaxation to clients suffering from post-traumatic stress or as an aid to de-sensitization of phobic reactions. The adoption of meditative techniques originating in Eastern spiritual traditions has expanded and deepened the practice of CBT, linking it with transpersonal approaches to psychotherapy.

Cognitive-behavioural approaches to psychotherapy and counselling are usually well thought through and available to revision and change. Their overall aim is to relieve human beings of distress, in the most demonstrably effective way and in the shortest time possible. This admirable objective can, however, lead to an over-emphasis on rapid external change, leaving some clients feeling that their deepest feelings have not been heard or met in the therapeutic relationship. The techniques themselves can be experienced as mechanistic and delivered in a directive fashion, especially in the case of 'homework', which can in itself evoke responses of dependent compliance or self-defeating rebellion. Interestingly, this orientation has, without advertising the fact, tended to espouse an ideal of human potential and the good life, which is not dissimilar to humanistic convictions regarding self-actualization.

Integrative psychotherapy approaches

These approaches are difficult to group together and may not yet be seen as a distinct theoretical orientation. There are some specific approaches that have explicitly drawn upon some of the theoretical concepts and methods of practical application nested within one or more of the three other orientations. The aim of this has been to provide what is held to be a distinct and more holistic approach to psychotherapy provision. A successful example would be cognitive-analytic therapy (Ryle 1990), which combines the active intellectual engagement of cognitive therapy with the explanations and insights of psychoanalytic psychotherapy. Some so-called integrative models of therapy are designed by an individual therapist, or group of therapists, and claim to include all the necessary ingredients for successful psychological therapy. These 'models' are put forward as having arrived at an approach that could, in theory, supersede the therapeutic approaches from which the individual concepts were derived. It is our view that there is a contradiction in terms concealed in the concept of an established 'model' of psychotherapy integration. Integrative psychotherapy, as a movement within the profession, can be understood as an ever-increasing body of knowledge about the over-arching theoretical concepts and the generic nature of psychotherapy practice. This movement provides an ongoing influence through which individual practitioners evolve their own integrative approach to their work, using a combination of theories and methodologies, which harmonize with their own belief systems and their wish to meet their clients' needs. Ideally, this activity involves them in a continuing process of assimilation and amalgamation as they arrive at their own creative and temporary formulations regarding the work. This view of the integrative psychotherapy movement is of a collection of individuals, highly motivated to find an ever-fuller response to the demands of their clients, and to include and explore all creative innovations in the field. Fundamental to this conceptualization is the conviction that no single approach to psychotherapy, however integrative, can fulfil these aims. Sadly, there seems to be a human need to arrive at a definitive answer and to claim superiority for one particular mode of response.

This process of integration can also be carried out within the established models of psychotherapy, contained by one of the overall orientations described above. Typical examples of this type of integration can be seen in the development of three major models of therapy practice: transactional analysis (TA); the more recent relational psychoanalysis; and cognitive behavioural therapy. TA has from the outset combined the insights of psychoanalysis with the educational and contractual aspects of behaviour therapy, while remaining firmly humanistic in its convictions regarding human self-actualization. New theories and methodologies developed within TA have been kept within the fold as different TA schools, allowing this approach to assimilate and invent newly formulated ideas without losing its overall objectives described above. In this manner it is quite usual for TA insiders to distinguish three main 'schools' within TA: the 'classical' school which has stayed close to Berne's original precepts with the aim of increased understanding leading to behavioural change; the 're-decision' school developed by Goulding and Goulding (1979) which incorporated emotion inducing techniques from gestalt therapy in order to achieve life changing re-decisions; and the 'cathexis' school which aims for the severely damaged client to have a completely new experience of growing up healthily through re-parenting by the therapists concerned (see Stewart and Joines 1987: 274–7). More 'schools' have been developed within TA but they would all maintain that they share an aim of assisting clients to achieve their full potential as adult human beings.

A similar process has taken place, to some extent, through the proliferation of different schools within the psychodynamic/psychoanalytic approach, although the level of integration of learning from outside of this orientation has rarely been acknowledged. A recent example of this type of integration, presented as new thinking based on professional experience, is the development of relational psychoanalysis (Mitchell and Aaron 1999), which makes the congruence of the therapeutic relationship central to the healing process and almost an objective in itself. The probable debt owed to the existential-humanistic approach for this innovation has not been fully acknowledged. This use of the non-verbal interaction is in agreement with the neuroscience research of Schore (2001) mentioned earlier.

Similarly CBT has developed theories regarding the importance of conditions of worth within the therapeutic relationship and including the need to explore childhood experience, without overt acknowledgement of the preoccupations of the Rogerian person centred therapy and the psychoanalytic schools of practice, especially the theoretical position of object relations therapists. Theoretical and technical developments, like Linehan's (1995) dialectical behaviour therapy (DBT), which is mentioned in the previous section, have integrated ideas from a very wide range of therapeutic orientations and even from spiritual teachings. Nevertheless, the professional field in which these new developments are acknowledged and contained remains CBT and integration with other approaches has not been encouraged, in spite of Wachtel's (1977) seminal text on the integration of psychoanalysis and behaviour therapy.

The objectives of integrative psychotherapists are, above all, to provide an effective service to their clients, which can help them to achieve their own aims, whether these are relief from emotional pain and dysfunctional behaviour or the actualization of their full potential as human beings. This means that the outcomes sought are less likely to be shared across all practitioners of this approach, who may differ in their belief as to the importance of increased insight or their ideals regarding self-actualization and existential authentic living.

Increasingly, integrative psychotherapists have become interested in what have been called the 'common factors' in all successful psychotherapy interventions (Goldfried 1980, 2003). Bohart and Tallman (1999) argue that the client is actually the main common factor as his or her own potentially active self-healer. In their view, a motivated and engaged client will select any cogent rationale given by the therapist and use whatever technique is offered. This does not mean that a principled integrative psychotherapist can use any or all techniques, or draw on any theoretical explanation. The approaches used and the creative innovations explored need to be harmonious with the practitioner's own belief system and within their capabilities. This means that integrative therapists have to know the limitations of the training they have received so far, and the scope of their own personal style of interaction. Some integrative therapists who are more eclectic in their approach aim, like Lazarus (1985), to skilfully use a wide range of techniques within a structured framework while holding to an over-arching theory of change. This is very different from the over pragmatic application of a haphazard collection of techniques, unsupported by a cogent theory of change. It is this danger of an ungrounded, superficial and muddled approach to psychotherapy that is most often cited as a criticism of the integrative psychotherapy approach. Perhaps the integrative practitioner has, more often, to face the existential truth that there is no one way to proceed in life, or in therapy work, and that there are no externally given meanings.

Concluding remarks

We have found ourselves, in the writing of this chapter, left with some issues arising from the objectives and outcomes as expressed within a professional field of differing theoretical orientations and a wide range of practical applications. We share, below, some of our discussions.

Jenifer
I realize that we have not included in this chapter many so-called 'models' of psychotherapy, in the belief that most of these are likely to be subsumed under the four main orientations described. However, we may need to ask ourselves specifically about body orientated psychotherapies, the more expressive arts based therapies and the so-called 'alternative' or complementary health therapies. Are the aims and objectives of these therapies likely to differ from those of the approaches which we have named as the main orientations? Surely the improved individual welfare of the client is the over-arching aim, although increased physical health and vitality and personal creativity might be seen as the initial objectives. What do you think?

Gabrielle
The expressive arts based therapies are very important because they meet the needs of people for whom words are a barrier and those who use words to ward off feelings. They recognize that

feelings are caught up in what we see and create and in how we move. Interestingly the body based therapies have developed approaches that are suitable for people who live predominantly in their bodies (proprioceptive) and those who live predominantly in their head (cognitive). Their aim is to repair the balance so that both ways of functioning are used (Totton 2003). My sense is that these therapies have very similar over-arching outcomes to the four theoretical groups mentioned in this chapter but achieve them in a different way. Broadly I think of them all being part of the existential-humanistic school with a considerable focus on wholeness and overall well-being achieved through using both the right and left brain functions. It leaves me wondering whether the more talking based therapies do also use brain function from both sides of the brain by making the therapy a creative activity. The therapist and client are in a creative process in which they play together to find out who someone is. In other words creativity does not have to be an activity in which an object is created but can be one in which ideas are created. This is reflected in the psychodynamic tradition, particularly in Winnicott's use of the word 'play' (1971).

Jenifer
We have also not discussed the criticism of the aims and goals of humanistic psychotherapies in that the ideals of these therapies have been formulated within a Western cultural context. They have been accused of an emphasis upon individual materialistic well-being rather than the importance of community and family group welfare. Even more significant might be the influence of this outlook upon social life and attitudes to the environment in general. If the aim of these therapies is to promote personal growth, how much of this might be construed as narrow self-interest and self care?

Gabrielle
The criticism that the ideals of humanistic based therapies are culturally bound and suited to Western cultures is also made of the psychodynamic, cognitive behavioural and integrative therapies. They all have objectives and desired outcomes which focus on the individual rather than the communal group. For instance it is hard for a Western trained practitioner to understand that seeing the head of a group rather than the

individual in trouble could bring about change for this latter individual. In Maori communities this is what the therapist may be asked to do. This challenge is being responded to in New Zealand by adapting the way of working. Narrative therapy (developed by Western therapists) has become popular in New Zealand because it has been possible to adapt it to offering something more appropriate to the Maori culture. I suspect other therapies are also going to need to change, and some of the ethical guidelines from counselling and therapy associations will also have to be reviewed. For instance some of the strict rules about dual relationships are culturally based (Syme 2003) and are not practicable in more communally based societies.

I wonder if the focus of the therapists on the individual in Western cultures has been necessary because so many people (the therapists included) had upbringings that were repressive and dominated by religious ethics of behaviour with a strong emphasis on guilt. I am not sure whether the selfishness and the need for instant gratification seen in Western cultures can be blamed on the therapeutic movement with its objectives of self-awareness and self-care, which at its worst can lead to self-centred and selfish behaviour. I believe that the therapeutic objectives were a response to societal needs at the time they were formulated, and not that they are a cause of societal problems. My worry is where will this end? Am I outdated, or is the permissive parenting that some therapists have encouraged damaging to society, and should the setting of boundaries, stressed so much by psychodynamic therapists, be more strongly emphasized to develop a more 'integrative' attitude in society?

Gabrielle
Psychodynamic approaches do seem to be more pessimistic about human nature and the expected outcome of therapy. I am reminded of Freud stating that the aim of therapy was to help clients move from 'neurotic misery to ordinary human unhappiness' (Breuer and Freud [1895] 1974); although he did on another occasion suggest that another aim was to restore the 'capacity to love and work' (Freud 1926). Do you think there are two life views within psychotherapy, just as you see in Christianity, where some believe in original sin and others in the innate goodness of human beings?

Jenifer
I think that this is the most interesting difference between orientations that has emerged from this chapter. Focusing upon objectives and outcomes has meant that we have constantly had to consider what are the over-arching belief systems held by an approach and whether this is consistent with the objectives as revealed by the methodologies used. For instance, the development of relational psychoanalysis may indicate a much more optimistic humanistic belief in human potential, as realized through a focus upon the authentic components of the therapeutic relationship. RET has a pessimistic view regarding human potential for growth and change, which it shares with the classical Freudian psychoanalytic approaches to therapy, unlike most of the other cognitive behavioural therapies that are designed to release clients from specific disabling psychological symptoms so that they can move towards a fulfilling good life. Even within the existential-humanistic orientation, there are some approaches that hold to the original European views of human existence as intrinsically challenging and difficult, requiring the 'courage to be' (Tillich 1952). The optimistic vigour of gestalt psychotherapy and the warm expectations of person centred therapy are in contrast with this emphasis. The range of theoretical views as to human potential seems to me to be broad and graduated between 'original sin' and 'innate goodness' rather than being clearly differentiated between orientations.

Gabrielle
Human potential seems to be important to therapists. Maybe this is because of our own lifestories. Some people suggest that all theories and their related objectives simply reflect the lifestory and psychopathology of the originator. Do therapists also choose orientations for the same reasons or do you think there is more chance than choice in the theory which a practitioner uses to inform their work?

Jenifer
Intuitively I would wish to respond that it is the philosophical belief system and the personality traits developed by therapists in response to their lifestories that shape their choices regarding training in a particular orientation. Yet it would be foolish to rule out the chance elements influencing these choices, arising

from the context within which they are made, the financial situation or even the literature read. In running workshops for therapists to find out more about their personal theories and styles as practitioners, I have noticed that questions about their views on the desirable outcome of therapy often reveal a belief system which belongs to a different orientation from the one the therapists have overtly espoused. (Elton Wilson 1993)

Gabrielle
In thinking about the next chapter, where we look at the different contexts in which psychological theories are practised, I am aware that the issues that bring clients to therapy rarely bear any relationship to the objectives of the main theoretical groups that we have looked at in this chapter. Most therapists work with people because they want them to be happier and have more fulfilled lives. How do they line up their clients' stated aims with their theoretical objectives?

Jenifer
Well, if most therapists are fundamentally well intentioned in their motivation, as you suggest above, then the more conservative views as to outcome may be held theoretically rather than pragmatically. I have become increasingly interested in motivation as the most significant factor influencing the effectiveness of psychological therapy, in any context and whatever the therapeutic approach being offered. Embedded in the motivation of both therapist and client are the beliefs they hold between them. The danger is that there is a mismatch or covert disagreement about possible objectives, particularly where therapists are wedded to their own value-laden ideas regarding the needs of their clients. An obvious example would be where the clients wants to make decisions in the here and now about a personal relationship while the therapist wants the client to explore their deeper issues arising from the past. Conversely a CBT therapist would naturally focus on the immediate problem and may not notice that at this time a particular client may need to explore their lack of self-esteem even in the counselling relationship.

Jenifer
CBT has made brief therapy a central concern of the therapist but the length of therapy is very important to most clients. This

may be why at the beginning of the twenty-first century, each orientation seems to have developed its own version of brief therapy. We have not really discussed in this chapter whether this has implications for the ideals on outcomes held by any of the theoretical approaches. I have noticed, in my reading and in many training situations, that attitudes to the duration of therapy vary widely between orientations. Humanistic approaches struggle with any form of time limit since it imposes an external condition upon what should be an organismic process of self-development. Even TA, which was originally designed by Berne to 'fix' the problems presented as soon as possible, has moved over the years to a preference for long-term therapy in order to complete the full healing process. Psychodynamic approaches have, in Malan's (1975) view developed a belief in the intrinsic superiority of long-term therapy and yet have an impressive number of innovators of radical forms of brief therapy. CBT has, from the outset sought an efficient and swift resolution of problematic issues. I wonder whether the necessity for brief therapy in so many contexts will prove to be an integrating factor between orientations as far as shared objectives and outcomes are concerned. And what might be the shared objectives of brief therapy?

Gabrielle
Originally psychoanalysis was brief. Over time it became longer and longer and therefore very expensive and so limited to relatively few people. Many of the brief therapies were developed in response to this situation. It is clear to me that these therapies can achieve the client's objectives with a satisfactory outcome. This has been an important and useful challenge to all practitioners. The strength of the brief therapies is that the objectives really have to be identified and the practice scrutinized for the outcomes to be achieved. I think this has resulted in considerable integration of technique if not of theory. It will be interesting to see if there is a gradual development of objectives that are perhaps less theoretical and more realistic. The more realistic objectives might be based on clients' real life goals rather than the somewhat idealistic theoretical goals commonly espoused by therapists.

CHAPTER **3**

Different contexts of psychotherapy provision

Introduction

As the original form of psychotherapy and counselling, psychoanalysis was first practised exclusively in private or independent practice, but nowadays the contexts for psychological therapy are very varied. Linked to the many contexts are a diverse range of objectives and a variety of expected or acceptable outcomes for both clients and therapists. It is also important to remember that the employer of the therapist may not be the client, but an agency, a medical care organization, an employee assistance programme (EAP), a school, a further or higher education college or university, a commercial business, the police force and so on. This means that the employer's preferred outcome has to be considered alongside that of the client. In situations where the counsellor is a volunteer the clinical responsibility for the client and the stated objectives will be those of the voluntary agency. The stated objectives and expected outcome can also vary considerably where the therapy setting is group work, family therapy or couple work. Telephone counselling and Internet counselling provide a new and expanding context for psychotherapy practice and it has been suggested (Strenger 2003) that a whole new client group, a 'generation x' or 'boho' (bourgeois bohemians) social group have arrived on the scene, looking for instant gratification of their therapeutic needs and uninterested either in examining the past or in any form of contractually based therapeutic relationship with the therapist. This challenging context may need to be considered separately from all others and is examined in our concluding discussion.

It is, in any case, rare for therapists working in any particular agency or organizational setting to be of a single theoretical orientation, except in some voluntary agencies that train their own volunteers. Therefore the therapist's personal objectives for the therapy and outcome for the client, derived from their theoretical background, may well have to be adapted to the context in which they work and possibly superseded by the employer's objectives.

In the previous chapter we discussed the main theoretical orientations, each with their stated objectives. These objectives are likely to be different from those of the clients and employers of therapists, who arrive with very varied goals or problems. Examples are:

- Survival through support
- Symptom control or cure
- Guidance in decision making
- Reduction in absenteeism and a return to work
- Harassment in the workplace
- Improving the capacity to study; passing exams; completing a course
- Working through a life event such as bereavement, infertility, injury, redundancy, divorce, sexual or physical abuse
- Personality and relationship difficulties; insight and understanding of self and others
- Sex therapy
- Dependency and addiction problems
- Crisis intervention and management
- Finding a meaning to life

Clients are likely to bring any of these goals or problems to therapists in private practice, even the work related aims, since EAPs usually refer their work based clients to private practitioners. The therapist has to decide whether he or she feels qualified to work with the goals presented and if not decide to refer the client, where this is possible. Some of these goals are more likely to be brought to a therapist in a particular setting or with special training. For instance improving the capacity to study is likely to be an issue brought to a therapist in a school, college or university. Sex therapy is likely to be brought to a therapist who is a trained sexual therapist and advertises as such, or to a voluntary agency such as Relate which selects and then trains volunteer therapists in sex therapy techniques.

It is clear that this list of client's objectives or goals is a long way from the stated objectives of the main theoretical orientations described in the previous chapter. The question in this chapter is how practitioners in these different settings alter their own theoretical objectives to meet the stated goals of clients, or the more hidden intentions of the employing organization. Do clients alter their goals to accommodate the therapist? These issues are addressed through considering the main contexts in which therapy takes place.

Psychological therapy in medical settings

In Britain, and perhaps in most Western countries, people are likely to seek help first from a medically qualified practitioner when they find themselves suffering from unbearable psychological distress, particularly when this state of mind is rendering them unfit to work or to function adequately in their family lives. Their objective is to have the pain removed, just as they would want a painful limb or organ cured by the medical practitioner. General practitioners are very rarely qualified as counsellors or psychotherapists, although they may back up their medical advice with counselling skills and offer some initial supportive counselling before referral to an in-house counsellor, secondary mental health services or to a therapist in private practice. Mental health practitioners whose qualifications to provide psychological therapy are immediately acceptable in a medical setting include psychologists, psychiatrists, psychiatric nurses or social workers and some psychotherapists. Many counsellors and psychotherapists working in medical settings are, however, not qualified through an interaction with medicine but are accredited as professional experts in the field of mental health.

Primary mental healthcare is almost always located in a general practitioner's (GP) surgery and takes the form of counselling sessions with individuals referred by their doctors to the practitioner employed by the practice for this purpose. This practitioner may be qualified as a psychotherapist, as a clinical or counselling psychologist or as a counsellor, but he or she is likely to be described as a counsellor rather than as a therapist. There has been a rapid increase in the provision of counselling by practitioners employed directly by GP practices although some counsellors conduct their private practices within the same building and are available for referrals.

In referring clients to the practice counsellor, doctors and nurses may have specific objectives, not necessarily matched by those of the counsellor. The doctor may want the counsellor to calm down or reassure an anxious client who has been making increasingly frequent visits to the consulting room. The doctor or nurse might expect the counsellor to make available a 'treatment' package to the client and then provide detailed feedback. The counsellor will want to offer the client a high level of confidentiality so as to facilitate trust in the therapeutic process. Conversely, the counsellor may want to liaise with the doctor regarding the use of medication yet find that prescriptions are being increased or decreased without consultation. The counsellor or therapist is likely to be influenced by their theoretical orientation and their learnt views about the 'medical model', which could include an over-respectful attitude to the medically qualified.

Is there an over-arching difference between counsellors and medical personnel? Do doctors and nurses want above all to save lives and improve physical health while counsellors are more interested in healthy social interactions and levels of self-development? All these issues need to be thought through and, ideally, discussed in the practice setting since it cannot be assumed that they have been considered in any depth in the setting up of a counselling service within a primary care setting. In order to make and retain good professional relationships with those referring clients to them, primary care counsellors and therapists usually benefit from offering explanatory and educational seminars and literature about counselling to all their colleagues, the receptionists and practice nurses as well as the doctors themselves. Other possible activities that primary care counsellors can provide are stress relief clinics and other forms of group work.

Clients seeking counselling within a primary care setting may have chosen this route because they see their psychological distress as a medical problem. In the UK people are accustomed to turning to the NHS for treatments which are free at the point of delivery, respectable and medically approved. Seeing a counsellor has become a more acceptable activity, mentioned regularly on television and radio, from news bulletins to soap operas. More GP practices are recognizing this demand and are able to refer a patient to the practice counsellor (where the patient may then be called a client, perhaps indicating a different outlook). However, like other treatments, counselling is usually offered on a time limited basis. The client may not be too concerned about this aspect of the service offered if he or she seeks some form of instant remedy to their distress. However, many counsellors are still being trained in forms of therapy which extol long-term and ongoing counselling commitments, and which seek to help clients achieve fundamental changes in insight and emotional responses. Currently, a number of courses in effective short-term therapy are being made available, usually as an additional module to the basic training course.

Primary care counsellors could benefit by matching their approach to clients to that of the experienced general practitioner, who sees patients when the need arises, provides as effective an intervention as is possible and then remains available for a return visit. Peake et al. (1988: 13) describe the psychotherapist as 'a healer who makes interventions at symptomatic junctures in the life cycles of individuals and families'. Their goals might then match to some extent those of their clients who seek to return to the stresses and strains of their everyday lives with less distress and perhaps more understanding of themselves. The practitioner skilled in brief therapy needs to discern what is needed from the current work to achieve this aim with a particular client, and to use the therapeutic alliance to encourage and motivate their clients to engage in the psychological movement demanded by this particular stage of their own journey. Clearly, this means offering a time focused therapeutic alliance rather than an immediate remedy and, in this way, differentiating counselling from the purely medical treatments offered by other practitioners within the primary care setting. Some clients may be motivated to continue their journey of self-discovery through a referral to private practice, while others may need to be referred on to secondary care. This latter option is more problematic since there is often a long period of waiting before this referral can take place, and many clients feel stigmatized by their encounter with psychiatric care.

Secondary care takes place under the administration of a hospital and the provision of psychological therapy is part of mental health care. Secondary care practitioners might work with patients in any of the following arenas:

- hospital out-patient clinic
- day hospital
- psychiatric ward
- psychotherapy department

In these settings practitioners may be described as psychotherapists, although the psychological therapy can be provided by counsellors, psychiatric nurses and social workers, as well as clinical and counselling psychologists and psychiatrists. Usually all these people have had a training in psychological therapy and are likely to espouse a particular model of psychotherapy within a theoretical orientation. This may sound an ideal situation but the levels of qualification and length of experience are likely to differ widely between practitioners. Often a psychiatric nurse has a wealth of experience regarding the behaviour of mentally distressed and disturbed clients but very little theoretical knowledge regarding the likely causes for the disturbance. Conversely, a psychiatric registrar may have attended a large number of seminars and case presentations aimed at achieving a correct diagnosis but lack any training in the basic therapeutic skills needed to establish a trusting working alliance. In addition, an accredited psychotherapist or counsellor might have trained and qualified in a non-medical setting but lack experience of the medical context and so they risk feeling disempowered, alienated and critical of the care which the client is receiving. All these factors can influence attitudes to objectives and outcomes.

In psychiatric settings a team approach is almost always promoted, which entails cooperation between a therapist and the other members of the staff that are interacting with their client. This means that discussions as to the desired goals of the therapy are not exclusive to client and therapist but can be also shaped by, for example, the views of the psychiatrist overseeing the work, the psychiatric social worker or art therapist involved in that particular case. While this team involvement can be supportive and reassuring, particularly where a client is engaged in suicidal or self-damaging behaviour, it can also lead to conflict and the danger of some form of defensive manipulation within the therapeutic alliance. Another danger is the general lack of optimism regarding outcome often found within psychiatric settings. Secondary mental health practitioners have often been disillusioned both by the experience of 'revolving door' patients who continually return to psychiatric care and by the institutionalization encouraged by a welfare benefit system reliant on a diagnosis of mental illness. Here again, client and therapist might benefit by formulating realistic aims towards achievable outcomes suited to the stage of personal development of the individual client work, rather than promoting some sort of medical 'cure'. The danger of psychiatry being perceived as the agency through which people are socialized into conforming is still an issue years after the original anti-psychiatry movement (Laing 1960; Szasz 1962, 1974; see also the companion volume in this series by Davies and Bhugra 2004). Counsellors and psychotherapists influenced by humanistic theory are likely to seek to empower their clients by encouraging them to develop their own individualistic aims, whatever the cultural pressure of their family and community. Conversely, more politically aware practitioners may dispute this focus upon the individual as implying that they have total responsibility for their own psychological problems, arguing that the problems might have been the inevitable result of social injustice (Pilgrim 1993).

Practitioners working within a medical context are likely to be faced with challenges to many of their personal assumptions regarding the overall objectives of psychological therapy and their role within the healing professions. Clients receiving counselling or psychotherapy through medical referral may be faced with an apparent dissonance between their expectations of an externally provided curative outcome and their therapist's promotion of psychological work within a therapeutic alliance. The influence of the context is indisputable.

Workplace counselling

In the past 15 years it has become much more common for employers to provide counselling for their employees. In this setting 'counselling' is the most usual term used. Perhaps this is because of a wish to avoid suggesting that people are ill or disturbed in seeking help. The range of employers providing counselling for their staff is very varied: examples are commercial businesses, educational institutions, national and local government offices, hospitals and religious organizations.

They may employ one or more counsellors, depending on the size of the operation, or they may subcontract the work to an EAP, which enlists and employs the counsellors. There are considerable differences for counsellors employed directly by a business or organization, as opposed to working for an EAP. In the former a counselling service may be placed in the occupational health or the human resources department and the counsellors are likely to be much more aware of the employer's policies, ethos, business aims and needs. These counsellors are often involved in staff development, running short training courses, taking part in management meetings and assisting in conflict resolution. As a result, they may have multiple roles and potential conflicts of interest, which have to be carefully managed. If an EAP is arranging the counselling, it manages the interface with the employer, which distances the counsellor, and can result in a counsellor being unconcerned about the objectives of the client's employing organization that is actually paying for the counselling. This distancing can be beneficial because it allows the counsellor to focus on the client exclusively, but if all awareness of the employer's needs is lost this can be detrimental to the client–employer relationship.

The main objective of the employers, however benevolent they may be, is ultimately an economic one; the desired outcome is the improved performance of their employees, who are likely to be more productive and work better when they are happy and not stressed either by work or personal problems. Current health and safety legislation has also to be observed. There have been some very high profile cases of employees successfully suing their employers for permanent ill health caused by excessive stress. These settlements are often very expensive and indirectly increase the overheads of the business. In some instances counselling is available because of the occupational risk of suffering from Post Traumatic Stress Disorder (PTSD). Examples are bank and building society employees who have been held at gun- or knife-point during a raid, or of fire crews, police and hospital staff who have seen appalling injuries as a result of major incidents. Other jobs such as those of airline pilots, train drivers, police and fire crews are extremely stressful because of the responsibility carried by one person or the high risk nature of the job. Counsellors are also often employed when people are being 'out-placed' or have been made redundant.

In all types of workplace related counselling there are three sets of objectives to be considered: those of the employer, those of the employee-client and those of the counsellor. Employees are likely to have sought help because they, or their peers or manager, recognize that their work is below par; such clients will probably know what problem(s) are causing their changed performance at work. Sometimes the problems are so severe that they have become ill and signed off work by their GP. One possible set of problems relate to work issues such as bullying, sexual harassment, relationship with colleagues or a manager, seeking promotion, feeling unrecognized or passed over for promotion, feeling over-worked or under-worked. In addition, clients are likely to bring to the counsellor a personal issue such as a relationship problem, a bereavement, a seriously ill member of the family, a mental health problem. This can result in two objectives: the objective of improving one's performance or returning to work, which are in line with the employer's purpose; and the objective of reducing a person's unhappiness, which is personal to the client. The counsellor has both of these objectives in mind together with any that arise from their own theoretical background, such as self-actualization or increased insight.

In this organizational context counselling is almost always short-term and time limited, typically 3–12 sessions, largely because employers are financing this service as part of an employment package and need to have budgetary control of their costs. The challenge for counsellors is to find a way within these time constraints to hold these differing objectives and reach an outcome that is satisfactory to all parties. This desired outcome might be an improved performance at work, or a return to work of the employee-client who has, as the result of counselling, increased insight into their difficulties, and more ego strength to face any further difficulties at work that remain. However, in reaching this outcome it is possible that the client's *work related* objectives have to be prioritized and therefore the focus is more on the major issues which are thought to be affecting performance. Other more personal issues are not unimportant and may need attention later; although sometimes a brief spell of counselling can give a client the tools to deal with the other issues without recourse to further sessions, or give them a good 'taster' of therapy so they decide to work with another therapist on the issues.

The actual outcome can be affected adversely or beneficially by the method of referral. Self-referral is the norm, but managers are often encouraged to suggest to their staff when counselling might be helpful and some managers contact the counsellor on behalf of their staff. The relationship of the manager with a staff member and the way in which the referral is made can affect the outcome.

The question posed in this chapter is whether counsellors can achieve a satisfactory outcome for all three parties without altering their theoretical objectives. Or do the clients alter their goals to accommodate those of the counsellor? In practice most counsellors have an ideal aim for their work, such as promoting insight, enabling self-actualization or helping client reach their full potential. At the same time, counsellors align themselves with a client's stated goal, which might be coming to terms with a death, no longer being depressed or improving their performance at work. Thus counsellors do not alter their fundamental objectives but rather look for realistic as well as idealistic goals. This means that some of a client's goals can be achieved, although perhaps not all, obviating the need for clients to alter their goals. As a result clients, whose introduction to counselling is in the workplace, are both surprised that most experienced counsellors are realistic and not 'airy-fairy' (a common prejudice, particularly in the business world) and satisfied to find that counselling has made a difference. But if counsellors are unable to relinquish their theoretical ideals, counselling in the workplace is very frustrating, with the consequence that no one's objectives are achieved.

Counselling in educational settings

Counsellors are employed by schools, colleges of further and higher education (FE and HE) and universities. This is another context in which the term 'counselling' is used rather than 'psychotherapy' and for the same reasons as in the workplace. The rationale behind the employment of counsellors, shared by the counsellors themselves, is that learning is adversely affected by emotional difficulties. For young people in transition, a therapeutic intervention at an early stage can prevent more severe emotional problems developing. There is also an economic rationale for FE and HE colleges and universities, which is that the funding of courses is dependent on numbers. If people drop out of courses, the courses are threatened with closure and staff may be made redundant. For schools an additional rationale is that bad behaviour and absenteeism are signs of emotional upset. The reputation of the school is often based on their handling of behaviour problems and their record for absenteeism. Therefore the reduction of these two problems is an additional objective in employing counsellors. As with workplace counselling, there are therefore three sets of objectives: those of the educational staff (representing the employer), those of the pupil or student and those of the counsellor. For the younger children there may also be the objectives of parents or carers to consider.

In institutions of further and higher education, the objectives of the staff are twofold. The administrative group have an economic concern, and the teachers, tutors and lecturers are concerned with the students' capacity to learn and with their performance in examinations, as well as the retention of students. Of course, there is also concern for the anguish of some young people. Students are likely to be concerned about their performance and the stress caused for some by the pressure to pass examinations; but they may also present with issues arising from their family, such as their parents fighting, the death of a member of the family, or homesickness, and personal issues such as sexual orientation, or their relationships; all of which can interfere with learning. Some students bring into the educational setting their memories of traumas experienced within the family, including issues of abuse. Counsellors in this setting, despite their ideal objectives arising from their theoretical orientation, will, as in the settings already referred to, tend to align themselves with the stated goals of their clients.

Usually this work is short-term, time related work, typically 4–12 sessions. An additional feature is that terms or semesters and the routine of examinations shape the work and influence the problems brought by students. Counsellors may meet some of the educational institution's objectives by running short courses on topics such as study skills, stress management, pre-examination groups, support groups for new students or training in listening skills so that students can support each other. In the counselling itself the presenting problem has to be held in mind and in most cases, the objective of the student to complete the course needs to be observed. The challenge is to do sufficient work on the presenting problem and the underlying emotional cause so as to enable the resumption of effective learning. In this situation the objectives of the educational establishment, the student and the counsellor come together. Another rather different example might be facilitating a three-way meeting, provided all parties agree, so that, a tutor and student can work out together why a particular assignment is so difficult.

However, counsellors may find themselves in conflict with teaching staff or the institution or both. An example of the former is if one of the counsellor's objectives is to foster the maturity of young people, whereas staff want the course work completed, the examination passed, and the number of course members retained. To this end tutors might set a deadline for handing in work and then extend it several times, whereas the counsellor might advocate no extension of the deadline to force students to take responsibility for the consequences of not meeting a deadline. Over-anxious tutors or those over-involved with students can cross boundaries because of their learning based objective of getting the student to complete assignments. This can again compromise the counsellor's objective of encouraging increased maturity.

There are occasions where the counselling results in the student becoming aware that their unhappiness, which brought them to counselling, is because they are in the wrong place. The facilitation of this discovery by the counsellor may result in the student leaving the college or university. Such an outcome is opposite to one of the objectives of the counsellor's employer and the tutors, which is to retain students.

The challenge of working in this context is one of capitalizing on the short-term, time limited nature of the work, and on the shape of the work imposed by terms and semesters; identifying the cause of the difficulty the student is having in studying and benefiting from being in a college or university; and then working on that issue in a focused way, trusting that other issues can be worked on later in the student's life. The danger can be of seeing many possible objectives which would be interesting and might result in self-actualization and increased insight for the student but are not appropriate to the context which primarily has learning objectives.

Much of this is also true of counselling in schools, but there are issues about objectives and outcomes that are unique to such establishments. The client age group is younger, ranging from 5 to 19 years, although in the United Kingdom there are very few counsellors in primary schools. Even in secondary schools the provision is patchy, with the presence of counsellors being the exception rather than the rule. The reverse is true in higher and further education. Work with young people under 16 is framed in the United Kingdom by the 1989 Children Act, which requires counsellors to consider the child's wishes and level of competence to make decisions. The rights and concerns of parents and carers of the children are also important, so the parents' objectives may need to be ascertained and then balanced against the child's or young person's objectives. This is where the level of competence of a child has to be considered, particularly if the parents' and carers' objectives are different from those of the child. It is important to gain, wherever possible, the parents' or carers' support for the counselling because the young people are dependent on these adults. Another feature of this work is that the counsellor may counsel more than one member of the family, either siblings or the parent(s) themselves.

Self-referral is less common with this age group, so the referrer (a teacher, parent or carer) may have objectives that the young person does not understand or accept. An example might be of a class teacher noticing and being concerned that a young person arrives at school very late every day, and suggesting that the pupil talks to the school counsellor. The pupil may well comply with the teacher's request but then be silent with the counsellor because of not wanting to reveal that her parents are drunk every morning, so she has to get her siblings dressed, give them breakfast and get them to their schools before coming to school herself. The silence might be because the young person has been led to fear 'the authorities' (social services) becoming involved or she may have been sworn to secrecy. This type of interaction has to be handled with immense sensitivity. Children and young people may also resent the interference of the referring adult, which might make the forming of a therapeutic alliance impossible. If the counsellor recognizes this resentment and enables the young person to express it, the therapeutic work may be able to proceed towards the desired outcome.

As in other settings counsellors have to bear in mind the school's objectives as well as those of the client, in this case those of the child or young person. A possible difficulty for counsellors who have been teachers is that they might be more concerned about the school's objectives than the child's. An example might be a child who is causing chaos in the classroom because of bad behaviour. This might result in the counsellor paying more attention to the bad behaviour than the child's misery that is being acted out.

Sometimes the counsellor may have to help a child accept different outcomes, because children tend to be more concrete thinkers than adults. For instance they might state that what they want is for their divorced parents to come together again, or for their dead grandfather to come alive. The therapist's task is to understand this desire and help the child to accept that they can have a fantasy, that the fantasy will not come true, but that it is understandable and is about how awful their world has become.

In work in schools there are statutory obligations, under the Children Act, which cannot be ignored. It is also likely that the terms of employment make it mandatory to inform their employers or social services if physical or sexual abuse is suspected. This can result in a considerable conflict for counsellors between their therapeutic objective and their professional obligation. For example: a mother brings her son to a school counsellor, ostensibly because his latest report indicates that he is falling behind his peers and under-achieving. The boy tells the counsellor that he is unhappy because he has no friends and is teased by people in his class. In a session with the boy's mother it is revealed that he is being severely beaten by her husband, which fits in with the counsellor's perception that the boy appears cowed. The counsellor has a duty to report this to the school, which in turn has an obligation to involve the social services. The result can be that the mother feels a confidence has been betrayed, cannot trust the counsellor any more and terminates the counselling. The mother is then no longer getting the help which was one of the objectives of the counsellor. The boy may be removed from his parents so that, although his safety has been assured, the counsellor's objective of giving the boy a better school experience has been superseded.

One of the difficulties of work in schools is that the outcome may satisfy none of the parties involved. This is because there may be such conflict between the objectives of the school and those of the child, or between the child's objectives and those of his or her parents or carers, or between the objectives of all three parties. In these situations the objectives of the counsellor can be totally subverted and the work made impossible.

Counselling in these educational settings nearly always presents some challenges to the counsellor's own theoretical belief system, as demonstrated in these examples. The aim of increased insight and/or authenticity in their clients is severely limited by the dominance of academic aims and the power held by the clients' parents and tutors. Perhaps, at best, the student client can be offered a wider view of their potential through the counsellor's consistent focus on issues of personal choice and responsibility.

Psychological therapy in the voluntary sector

The provision of therapy in the voluntary sector can be split into two main groups: services with a focus on a specific problem, such as bereavement, relationship difficulties or addiction problems; and services offering generic therapy, some of which may be free or low cost at the point of delivery. The therapists in either case can be volunteers or paid. If they are paid it is usually below the going rate in that area, the agency itself often being a charity (drug and alcohol services are generally better funded than other charity services).

Many voluntary organizations providing counselling or psychotherapy are problem focused. Therapists working for these agencies may be entirely trained by the agency or have done a qualification in counselling or psychotherapy and then had specialist training from the agency. The agencies themselves will probably have an attitude to clients and an approach to client work which may be influenced by existential-humanistic, psychodynamic, integrative or cognitive-behavioural theory, but the prime focus is to assist the client with a specific issue. Of course, clients seek them out because these agencies advertise themselves as dealing with a specific issue. Examples of agencies in the United Kingdom are: Relate, which offers to work with couples with relationship difficulties; Cruse, which helps the bereaved come to terms with a death of a loved one; Compassionate Friends, which helps parents who have lost children, and MIND which offers counselling to people with mental health problems. In addition there are many local, rather than national, agencies specializing in specific issues such as rape, sexual abuse in childhood or supporting gay and lesbians to 'come out'. In some instances an issue such as institutional abuse has become such a problem that a nationwide counselling service has been established. This has occurred in Eire and Northern Ireland, and in Australia.

The result of being focused on a single issue is that the agency, the therapist and client have one objective in common, even if there are other issues that become clear during the therapy and might result in the desired outcome being unachievable. For example, a client might seek help coming to terms with the death of a partner, but it might become clear to the therapist, if not to the client, that the grief work is blocked because of multiple unresolved losses in childhood and so the outcome cannot be achieved. One of the tasks of a supervisor working for the agency is to help the therapist keep the focus on the grief work and if this becomes impossible because of the earlier history of the client, to facilitate referral elsewhere.

It can be more difficult for a common objective to be found and a desired outcome to be achieved for the agency, the therapist and the client where the client is a couple. The agency and the therapist might have as an objective that the two people work out whether they stay together or part, but the objectives of one member of the couple could be incompatible with those of the other. One partner, who is having a secret affair, might wish to leave the relationship with the current partner, whereas the other could be determined never to end the relationship because they believe that vows once made are inviolable. Unless these incompatible objectives can be modified to reach an objective that both members of the couple agree on, the outcome will be unsatisfactory for at least one party. Both the agency and the therapist are likely to have a realistic expectation that objectives and satisfactory outcomes are not always attainable, or only attainable if all parties agree on what they should be, but one or both of the couple could be deeply dissatisfied if they are not aware of this.

As with all other sectors the work can be short- or long-term but it will probably be shorter in the voluntary sector where there is a clear objective and focus to the work. Many of the volunteers are trained in short-term rather than long-term work. This focus on a tightly circumscribed outcome can be very satisfactory and rewarding for the therapist and client, because they are both seeking an achievable and realistic outcome. Conversely, the need for a short time limit can seem inappropriate where the focus issue of the agency is linked to a wide range of problems, such as those surrounding sexual abuse. Volunteers in these agencies are likely to have been trained in the belief that long-term work is needed for such clients. In these cases, the agency itself needs to be able to provide ongoing contact so that clients can return to counselling, perhaps with a different practitioner, at each stage of their journey towards recovery.

In recent years both MIND and Relate have branched out and had contracts with primary care trusts (PCTs) and health care trusts (HCTs) to counsel people with more general problems, and therefore these agencies have had more generic objectives. The main aim of agencies providing a generic form of counselling was, and often still is, to supply counselling to groups who are deprived, either because they are unemployed or have a low income, or do not have easy access to therapists in the independent sector. Where agencies are offering therapy to socially, emotionally and economically deprived people there are philosophical and altruistic objectives that underline the agency's work and are likely to be a motive behind the volunteers' desire to work in the agency. These objectives lead to the agency being registered as a charity and raising money to support work with clients who cannot fund their own therapy. Therapists usually work as volunteers, with no payment or they receive less than the going rate. Inevitably the number of sessions and the number of clients are controlled by the financial resources, by the demand in the area (such services easily become over-subscribed) as well as by the client's needs. Some agencies manage this dilemma by having sufficient fee-paying clients to cover the shortfall. In making assessments the therapists have to set a realistic fee with those who can pay: realistic to the agency's needs and the client's ability to pay. Some therapists find it very difficult to negotiate a large enough fee from those who have the means to pay, because they believe that therapy should be free or inexpensive for everyone, regardless of their need and ability to pay. Before working for a charity therapists therefore need to be sure of their own motives and accept the need for the service to be financially viable. Otherwise there is a danger that therapists can subvert the work of the charity and cause its collapse by negotiating fees that are too low or engaging in contracts that are too long.

This over-arching objective of these voluntary agencies affects the delivery but not the therapeutic objectives, which are likely to be closer to the clients' wishes than those of a theoretical orientation. This is because in most voluntary agencies the therapists are unlikely to have all been trained in one modality, unless the agency has trained them.

Pastoral counselling

This type of counselling is always done with an awareness of a
religious context and can be part of the priestly tradition of the
'cure of souls', confession, spiritual direction and healing. Many
pastoral counsellors are lay people, rather than ordained
ministers, who practise pastoral counselling in church affiliated
agencies or in independent practice. What they have in common
is that they take religious and spiritual problems seriously,
recognize that some clients bring deeper questions of meaning,
and that mind, body and spirit are all important aspects of being
human.

Pastoral counsellors are not of any one orientation but have
common objectives of healing, sustaining, reconciling, guiding
and nurturing (Foskett and Jacobs 1989). Healing has a similar
objective to that of many other therapists, which is to help
people live with themselves and the world more contentedly.
Sustaining is a supportive role; reconciling is seen in work with
couples, families or groups who are in conflict; guiding may
involve looking at vocational, work or marriage choices; and
nurturing as encouraging personal growth and development. It
can be seen that these objectives overlap with those of therapists
of every theoretical orientation and who work in all settings.
These objectives are also what people are seeking for when they
ask for counselling. What is distinctive is the explicit acknowledgement of a religious belief on the part of the counsellor,
which the client usually knows of when they seek help.

In recent years a different type of religious counselling,
Christian counselling, has emerged from evangelical Christian
churches. This differs from pastoral counselling in general
because there is a specific evangelistic aim, with the use of the
Bible to underpin the work and practices used such as the laying
on of hands and exorcism. The specific objective of evangelism
has resulted in some Christian counselling being disapproved of
by counsellors who believe that religious beliefs should only be
explored if they are introduced by the client. In addition, the
Christian emphasis on forgiveness can, on occasion, be
introduced inappropriately as a desired objective of the
counselling work. Here the counsellor's belief system and
evangelistic objectives may be thought of as potentially intruding
upon the client's own aims.

Concluding remarks

Jenifer
This chapter has explored the way context always shapes the nature of the therapeutic alliance, with implications for the goals set and the outcomes sought by client and therapist. Above all, I am left with a question about purpose, the overall purpose of psychotherapy as practised in a variety of contexts within a Western democracy. Is therapy in the service of the individual or of the environment in which it is provided? Educational settings and work settings provide free counselling for students and employees so that they can be released sufficiently from their distress to achieve the aims of the organization within which they study or work. Medical settings provide psychological therapies as part of a more general obligation to preserve the health of the individual within a community and, in the case of centrally funded health services, to fulfil the promise of healthcare free at the point of delivery. Voluntary agencies and religious foundations offer counselling in order to assist with specific problem areas or to make some form of talking and listening therapy available to people who fall outside other categories. It seems as though only in independent practice can the purpose of psychotherapy and counselling be truly free from other agendas and address the purpose of the individual client. And even in this context, the training, the assumptions and belief system of the therapist offering their services in private practice have to be taken into account.

Gabrielle
I am immediately reminded of John Donne's aphorism, 'No man is an Island, entire of it self' and that it is a luxury if not a fantasy to believe that therapists can work outside a context and without constraints.

The question of purpose of therapy and in whose service it is performed is an interesting one. What it makes me think about is that perhaps the overall task of therapy is to enable people to accept themselves within the environment in which they live and work. If this is the case then therapists need to be aware of the constraints in which they themselves live and work in order to model realism for the client. An employer holds the power and will not suddenly change; an unhappy employee has to find a way to live with this situation or leave. A personal relationship will not survive if one member does not wish to be there. In this instance the therapist has the task of helping the couple face the reality that the relationship is over.

I do not think therapy is in the service of any one person, employer or organization but rather that it is for the whole of society. I do not want to sound grandiose or idealistic but I believe that each generation of people work for their society to be a happier place than they perceived that it was before. The new profession of psychotherapy and counselling has had an increasing role in this during the late twentieth and early twenty-first centuries.

Jenifer
Staying with the previous issue, while the psychotherapy profession may share a general desire, 'for their society to be a happier place', I think there is a danger that psychotherapists conform to whatever is the current view regarding the 'good life'. I personally view psychotherapy as a much more subversive process, disturbing and questioning societal values as represented by the structures adopted and adapted to in childhood and used, outside of their awareness, by individuals to cramp their full potential as human beings. I think psychotherapy practitioners need to be cautious about their own adaptations to social pressure and avoid a subtle collusion with the authority and power of any particular context, be it in education, health, religion, politics or any other context. These thoughts seem to be linked with another issue. I notice that we have not explored two contexts which focused not only upon particularly problematic issues but are issues that are some of the most difficult to work through and resolve. These are the agencies focused on substance abuse therapy provision for convicted criminals in a prison setting. I am curious as to how we overlooked these settings and whether we have somehow excluded the excluded! In any case, I am aware that it is where any sort of antisocial behaviour is concerned that the objectives of the therapist might become aligned with society's requirements rather than with tracking the desired outcome of the client. These clients have to some extent opted out of mainstream society. They live on the margins and often seem to be protesting against societal norms with their behaviour.

Gabrielle

There are many more contexts for counselling or groups of clients we could have mentioned. Examples of other contexts are counselling within social work, in residential homes and services for women, asylum seekers and refugees, survivors of torture, sexual abuse or rape. Adding these to the contexts we have included would still not be a definitive list. These types of work we are now touching on are difficult because of the setting in the case of working in a prison, or because of the issue the client brings. For example, if a client has been tortured, the emotional damage and trauma are the focus of the work, with the aim of reducing or removing resulting symptoms, but the therapist needs specialist training to do the work and may well need extra supervision to deal with the impact of the horrific abuse that has happened to this fellow human being. Counselling perpetrators of crimes or abusers is another example of specialist work, where the therapists need out of the ordinary support, supervision and training. The crime may be abhorrent to the therapist; the danger is that this feeling makes the therapist punitive, with the result that the therapy is not restorative to the client.

Despite the difficulty of the work, working through the particular problem for which the client seeks help is likely to be the objective of the therapist and the client, as it is in other settings we have discussed. It may be that the methods of working learnt in association with a particular theoretical orientation might have to be reviewed. For instance psychodynamic practitioners might be reluctant to help an asylum seeker with housing issues because of the dual relationship formed, whereas this might not be such an issue for practitioners from other orientations.

Gabrielle

Thinking about what we have not discussed in this chapter brings me to my next concern. Although there are counselling agencies focusing on a huge range of problems and as well as many generic counselling services, I wonder whether some problem groups are missing out totally. Is counselling really available to people from the ethnic minorities or is it available but unattractive because it is culturally inappropriate to these minority groups? There are also wide areas of the country where there are very few counsellors or counselling services. The major providers are in large cities and towns and not in rural areas. It could be that telephone and online counselling will become increasingly important; perhaps more attention should be given to training in this area.

Jenifer
I agree with you that there are still large groups of people who find counselling and psychotherapy inaccessible. Often this is a matter of culture, education or perceived social class. Sometimes the demands of a person's daily life means that it is difficult to make time for private and personal discussion. I am thinking of mothers of very young children, of carers generally and of members of close family groups who are expected to account for every moment of their day. More and more people use the Internet or the telephone to meet their needs and I think providers of training in psychotherapy and counselling will indeed need to consider what skills and qualities will be required to use these new media effectively. I wonder what influence, if any, these contexts will have on the direction of the therapeutic work. At present, there is an assumption that telephone or online counselling is likely to be only an introduction to the therapeutic process. Many EAP and generic counselling agencies operate a telephone assessment service, which aims to provide an initial listening service and to direct the client towards the service that can be of most help. Other telephone helplines, such as the Samaritans, provide a listening ear but do not aim to offer counselling interventions or any explanations for the psychological distress being off-loaded. Many therapists find themselves offering one off sessions by telephone, by email or even by the use of mobile phone text, when their clients are in distant locations or in emergencies. All these provisions have in the past been considered somewhat secondary to the person to person meeting of minds and presences, and are not usually linked to notions of a goal or an outcome. Yet there is no reason why online or telephone counselling should not be productive in itself and fulfil the needs of the caller or the subscriber for insight, emotional relief and behavioural change. As already mentioned (Strenger 2003) the so-called 'boho' generation of creative, high-achieving, wealthy and relatively young people are looking for a completely new kind of therapy which is immediately available and which proposes that the self is subject to perpetual experiment, design and re-design, in

constant search for a truly authentic way of being. Although they are a minority, the needs of this outspoken and media conscious group could influence the aspirations of less privileged users of Internet counselling. The aim might move towards achieving psychological transformation in as short a time as possible.

Gabrielle
Throughout this chapter we often mention or allude to short-term therapy. I wonder whether the time has come for the generic training of therapists to be predominately in short-term therapy, and for long-term work to be a specialism or a further qualification. In most countries of the world counselling is problem focused and therapeutic counselling as practised in Great Britain is a rarity. The medical model of treatment where people ask when they have need and come back if the symptoms re-emerge or a new symptom appears may be healthier than involving people in years of therapy. Further support for short-term therapy is the research evidence that major change happens in the first few sessions (Howard et al. 1986; Barkham and Shapiro 1989). Has the time come to alter training?

Jenifer
My easy and immediate answer to this question is, 'Yes!' The research regarding the 'dose effect' of the first ten or so sessions is well supported and has been expanded to show that where therapy can continue for a year or more even more change is likely to take place, after a somewhat dormant period when as far as measurement change is concerned little seems to be happening. However, I am extremely cautious about the current swing towards a view that short-term therapy is always better and more effective. Whenever and wherever I am asked to train people in what I prefer to call 'time focused' psychological therapy, I always encourage choice and flexibility in the provision of counselling or psychotherapy. I am increasingly convinced that individuals have their own journey of psychological growth and evolution to work through. Sometimes they need only a short period of therapeutic interaction, but at other times they are willing to fund themselves through a much longer exploration of their patterns of thought, feeling and behaviour. The popular limitation of therapy to six sessions, usually promoted by financially motivated managers, has no particular research evidence to

support its widespread application where therapy is free at the point of provision. Perhaps training in accurate assessment of motivation and current need should precede an emphasis on training in short-term therapy. This brings us back to our fundamental questions about the importance of the aims and objectives of client and therapist, and the issue of what happens anyway!

Until recently, most psychotherapy training has been directed towards those planning to work in private practice. The external situation regarding career opportunities for trainees has changed, and most training institutes and courses are only gradually adjusting the character and content of their syllabus to fit in with these changes. There is a challenge to provide trainees with the tools to assess clients and manage contractual commitments that meet the actual objectives of their clients, often based on recent life events, rather than the ideals promoted by an over-arching theory of psychotherapeutic well-being. Perhaps this is particularly true for trainees planning to work within EAPs, medical settings or voluntary agencies.

CHAPTER **4**

Research on objectives and outcomes

Introduction

The words 'objectives' and 'outcomes' are usually seen to be terms commonly used by *researchers* into psychotherapy and counselling rather than by practitioners themselves. In this chapter, we intend to explore the concept of research as an activity that has explored, measured and reported upon the results of psychotherapy and has, inevitably, although in smaller measure, linked these results to the aims of the client and practitioner. A related purpose is to interest all practitioners of psychotherapy in the possibility of developing a research attitude to their own practice and of making practical use of research into objectives and outcomes to enhance and improve their practice. The particular standpoints of psychodynamic and humanistic practitioners are acknowledged and compared with the research based practice of cognitive behaviourist therapists. Inevitably, this involves some discussion of the reasons why there is a continuing evidence of a 'gap between psychotherapy practice and research' (Goldfried and Wolfe 1996), given that the outcome continues to be a major focus of psychotherapy research. We review, very briefly, the research literature relevant to our interest as practitioners in the aims and purposes of psychotherapy and its outcomes. It seems that practitioners are most interested in reading about *what works* and *how it works*, and so both outcome and process research are used to contribute to this exploration. Included in the discussion is an account of a small informal questionnaire based inquiry relevant to this subject area, carried out by means of a workshop presented to practitioners in different contexts.

Until recently, it was commonplace for researchers to remark upon the continuing lack of interest shown by most practitioners, regardless of their own approach to psychological therapy, in reading or using research findings in their day to day practice (Morrow-Bradley and Elliott 1986; Howarth 1988; Elton Wilson and Barkham 1993; Goldfried and Wolfe 1996). Volumes purporting to be 'complete guides' of psychotherapy contained only a cursory mention of research or evaluation (Kovel 1976; Corey 1986). This situation has changed to the extent that there seems now to be a concerted effort by a minority of scientifically minded practitioners to interest other practitioners in current and new paradigm research (Elton Wilson and Barkham 1993). Training programmes in psychotherapy are beginning to include research modules as standard (Elton Wilson 2000a), even outside psychology departments. A few journals are being launched and one or two books are being written which aim to be reader friendly and of interest to practitioners (McLeod 1999, 2001). Even experts in evidence based research trials can be seen to be interested in convincing and informing practitioners of the relevance of this work (Roth and Parry 1998; Rowland and Goss 2000). Qualitative research, although still criticized by the more concrete, proof-seeking thinker, is gaining respectability as an appropriate methodology for a profession heavily influenced by humanistic philosophy. Practitioners could be, and some are, encouraged by the indisputable fact that research into outcomes of psychotherapy carried out over the years has, on the whole, validated their profession (Luborsky et al. 1975; Wampold 2001):

the efficacy of psychotherapy has now been firmly established and is no longer a subject of debate

(Wampold 2001: 59)

More recently, rigorously controlled research studies into *counselling* as a specific branch of psychological therapy have endorsed this opinion (Mellor-Clark 2000). These studies expand the effectiveness argument to the counselling offered by trained practitioners in a primary care setting as being more likely to improve symptoms than routine GP care. However, the majority of these studies into the effectiveness of counselling and psychotherapy have been carried out by researchers external to practice contexts and do not seem to have encouraged practitioners involved in day to day work with clients to explore the effectiveness of their own work as it is carried out. Even as this book is being written, a senior UK clinical psychologist, Marzillier, with many years experience as a psychotherapy practitioner, has once again thrown down the gauntlet regarding the 'myth of evidence-based psychotherapy' (Marzillier 2004). He argues against the relevance of any form of evidence-based psychotherapy arising from outcome research which, in his view, 'does justice neither to the complexity of people's psychology nor to the intricacies of psychotherapy' (Marzillier 2004: 392). His attitude has disappointed and angered many other psychologist practitioners who promoted this type of research to their colleagues with the aim of making psychotherapy an acceptable treatment in the NHS.

Less open to validation has been the effectiveness of any one particular model of psychotherapy and it is a constant cause for wonder that the verdict of Lewis Carroll's Dodo Bird that '*everybody* has won and *all* should have prizes', as concluded by at least two major reviews of the relevant research (Rosenzweig 1936; Luborsky et al. 1975), has been ignored by so many of us practitioners, and by some researchers. We continue to ask researchers to find out 'what works for whom?' (Roth and Fonagy 1996). Perhaps this resistance to the notion of 'uniform efficacy' (Wampold 2001) is attributable to the attractive temptation for therapists to align themselves, however subtly, with an approach that claims to be superior to others in the field. The slow growth of an interest in demonstrating the 'common factors' (Grencavage and Norcross 1990; Frank and Frank 1991; Bohart 2000) as key to the understanding of effective psychotherapy practice is encouraging, but still limited to those bold enough to relinquish their own theoretical belief system. An exception to this is the generally accepted relevance of Truax and Carkhuff's research (1967) regarding the significant therapist qualities essential to the building and maintenance of the therapeutic relationship, whether sufficient (Rogers 1957) or simply necessary.

In preparation for this book, we have ourselves encountered an interesting example of this resistance with regard to our own questions about the purpose of psychotherapy, whether it is effective, how it works and in what context. Jenifer arranged a number of workshops billed as 'a shared exploration into the purposes and the consequences of therapy for client, for practitioner, for the immediate social system and for society at large' and entitled it 'The Impossible Enterprise?' (*Worth Reading!* 2003; SEPI Amsterdam 2004). These workshops were advertised according to the context, whether that was an international conference, an author event held by a therapy book club or as one of a series of workshops for supervisors. All these contexts were free of any focus on one particular approach to psychotherapy. In all cases there was a comparatively low level of attendance to the workshops, although those who did attend were interested, enthusiastic and evaluated the event positively. The feedback from organizers and from some of those attending was that they were initially put off by the subject matter and by the title. The use of any form of structured inquiry as a basis for the exploration of the objectives and outcomes of the therapeutic enterprise was appreciated only by those who were already prepared to ask some difficult questions about the practice of psychotherapy and their own participation in this activity. The findings from these workshops are described in more detail below.

So it seemed to us that, at least on an anecdotal level, many practitioners maintain a lack of personal interest or involvement in any type of formal research inquiry regarding the psychotherapy *outcomes* and *objectives* of their own practice. However, this lack of interest is challenged by an increasing demand on psychotherapy practitioners, particularly those employed by institutions, to justify and consider a formal evaluation of their practice, with a focus on clearly stated objectives and measurable outcomes. This demand has, ironically, arisen from the increased popularity of 'counselling', under which label consulting a practitioner of psychological therapy has been found to be more acceptable and attractive to the general public. Its popularity has alerted the mass media to what was a relatively obscure form of healing and it has attracted, in some cases, criticism and hostility to an apparently selfish and potentially harmful activity. At its most potent, psychotherapy can encourage individuals to question societal and cultural norms. In spite of this criticism, psychotherapeutic counselling has continued to be more widely sought outside of psychiatric settings and beyond the exclusive context of psychoanalytic practice. Recently public health services and health insurance providers have been drawn into the controversies about the usefulness of psychotherapy.

Historically, there has been a continuing cycle of outcome research that revisits, every decade or so, the following series of questions:

1 Is psychotherapy effective?
2 Which is the most effective therapeutic approach?
3 What therapeutic process affects outcome?

Is psychotherapy effective?

The first question regarding the effectiveness of psychotherapy was initially explored in depth in response to Eysenck's (1952, 1966) relegation of the curative claims of psychotherapy, with the exception of behaviour therapy, to the results of spontaneous remission. He argued that the same level of recovery from mental distress would take place whether people were treated by psychotherapy or left on a waiting list. A flurry of criticism and countercriticism of his methodology followed and a pattern was established of hostile and partisan claims and counterclaims (Rachman 1977; Bergin and Lambert 1978; Rachman and Wilson 1980; Lambert et al. 1986), which lasted until the early 1980s. Finally, the powerful findings of meta-analytic studies (Smith and Glass 1977; Smith et al. 1980) led to a generally accepted conclusion that psychotherapy's effectiveness had been firmly established, not least because it was shown to have deleterious effects in some cases, so Eysenck's original no-effect argument could be shelved. The general question of psychotherapy as a legitimate form of healing continues to surface from time to time and has been reasonably successfully upheld (Grissom 1996). In addition, corporate providers of psychotherapy have become highly motivated to find some objective justification for their funding of psychotherapy in general as an effective mental health intervention. One of the most convincing studies was a major investigation by *Consumer Reports* (1995) (the US equivalent of the magazine 'Which' produced by the Consumer's Association in the UK) that strongly supported the effectiveness of psychotherapy. Their survey covered 4100 respondents who had experienced some sort of so-called 'mental health' help. They concluded 'that patients benefited very substantially from psychotherapy, that long-term treatment did considerably better than short-term treatment, and that psychotherapy alone did not differ in effectiveness from medication plus psychotherapy' (Seligman 1995). More recently, in Britain, the Consumers Association has reported on the effectiveness of counselling in a general practice setting with results similar to those reported by Mellor-Clark (2000) above.

Which is the most effective therapeutic approach?

The initial question regarding psychotherapy effectiveness moved on rapidly to include the second question: *which is the most effective therapeutic approach?* As described above, meta-analytic studies into efficacy (Smith and Glass 1977; Smith et al. 1980) had already established what seemed to be the 'uniform efficacy' of all established psychotherapy treatments, and this conclusion, unpopular as it has proved to be with the proponents of competing models of psychotherapy, has been consistently replicated. However, from the earliest days there were some arguments that particular modalities of psychotherapy were better suited to particular mental disorders.

In order to compare psychotherapy approaches, a rigorous research methodology has been developed over the years, perhaps with too much reliance on the logic of the randomized clinical trial and the complexity of meta-analyses, which have been seen by practitioners as distant and alien to the rich experience of psychotherapy. In addition, a different terminology has been developed, in the general context of all evaluative research, to distinguish between highly controlled and often laboratory based *efficacy* research studies from *effectiveness* studies taking place in the context of applied practice. So it is become important to distinguish between psychotherapy *efficacy*, which indicates a conclusion drawn from comparing psychotherapeutic treatments with each other and with a 'no treatment' condition in a highly controlled context, and psychotherapy *effectiveness,* which refers to the benefits of psychotherapy occurring in a practice context (Wampold 2001: 60–1). While initially highly interested in the results of this type of enquiry, at least from the sidelines, those practitioners who read about research lost interest after the review by Luborsky et al. (1975) concluded that 'Everyone has won and all must have prizes', otherwise known as the 'Dodo Bird verdict', mentioned earlier in this chapter. This review of all the previous efficacy studies claimed that there are positive but broadly equivalent outcomes of diverse therapies, findings that were substantiated in later meta-analytic studies (Shapiro and Shapiro 1982). These meta-analytic findings continue to be replicated (Wampold et al. 1997) and yet claims for treatment or for modality superiority, particularly with regard to specific psychological complaints or the superiority of long-term therapy over short-term engagement continue to be explored. For instance, there are continuing claims and consistent findings (Roth and Fonagy 1996: 155–7) recommending that behavioural treatment with an added cognitive component, a form of cognitive behaviour therapy (CBT), is the optimum treatment modality for people suffering from obsessive compulsive disorder (OCD).

So the Dodo Bird effect (Luborsky et al. 1975), described above, has now been sidelined by a growing search for precisely targeted treatments for identifiable disorders, usually funded by the corporate providers of medical care, or, in the United States, by insurance companies faced with claims for psychological therapy treatments. These treatments, at least when subjected to structured research in the form of a random control trial, rely on set procedures, usually laid out in the form of manuals, to which practitioners are expected to adhere. The common factors, summarized by Seligman (1995) as 'rapport, expectation of gain, and sympathetic attention' pertaining to all potentially effective therapeutic approaches are labelled as *nonspecifics* and controlled against. In addition, the continuing difficulty in finding appropriate criteria for judging outcome in this complex field of human science is usually glossed over by researchers. Research of this sort necessarily takes place in controlled laboratory situations that are rarely applicable to the everyday context of psychotherapy practice. Technological approaches to psychotherapy, which are more easily adapted to the use of measurable change protocols in the form of behaviour and cognitive reports, are preferred. Other less easily specified approaches, particularly those that emphasize the quality of the therapeutic relationship in the form of a motivated contractual commitment, tend to lose out on the comparisons made. Practitioners of these therapies react either by ignoring these findings, or by joining the game of comparison and turning away from an interest in outcomes and focusing on an exploration of the process of therapy. In any case, some practitioners consider any overt emphasis upon outcome is likely to limit the subtle potential benefits of the therapeutic relationship.

Meanwhile, the vast majority of psychotherapy practitioners

have, continued to use their personal observation of change or growth in their clients as their only confirmation of effectiveness, either of their own approach or of psychotherapy in general. Asking clients for their opinion is still a process fraught with controversy, with many therapists asserting the possibility of harm to the therapeutic alliance or, conversely, affecting the transference. In addition, clients may wish to please or praise their therapists or even to covertly attack their therapist. Unfortunately, a practitioner's own observations may be laden with assumptions and a defensive need to prove their own worth or the effectiveness of their own theoretical and methodological approach. Research that compares the client's view of therapy with that of their practitioner at a process level has revealed surprisingly different views as to which was the significant event within a session (Elliott 1983; Rennie 1990; Elliott and Shapiro 1992; Elliott 1990) and has revealed the extent to which clients' experiences of therapy regularly differs from that described by practitioners.

What psychotherapy process affects outcome?

Historically, the move away from outcome research towards an interest in the third question listed above was, in some ways, a reaction to the earlier, somewhat anxious, search to validate psychotherapy as a worthwhile professional activity and then to demonstrate the superiority of one model of therapy. For a time, process research, as carried out and published by research minded practitioners, was looked upon as being of genuine practical use to the less scientifically skilled practitioner. Interpersonal process recall (IPR) (Kagan 1980), used as an aid to the form of grounded research carried out by Elliott (1983) and Rennie (1990), could even be replicated by practitioners through the use of a tape recorder and a neutral interviewer. IPR is a form of post-event interview where participants in the original event recall and discuss their recent experience in depth. However, the attention to complicated methodological detail and the language of grounded research could seem daunting and repetitive to many therapists. Yalom's work with his client, Ginnie Elkin, entitled *Every Day Gets a Little Closer* (1974) is a key example of a bold experiment in process research, linked to intermediate outcomes. Yalom and his client agreed to make notes at the end of every session and, at set intervals, exchanged these notes, thus sharing their observations and drawing conclusions as to the progress of the therapy. In contrast with the IPR based research mentioned at the end of the previous section (Elliott 1983; Rennie 1990; Elliott and Shapiro 1992), these conversations revealed similar as well as different views of the process, and through this methodology they enriched the process and progress of the therapy.

Almost all forms of process research involve the use of some sort of retrospective analysis of previous sessions, often backed up by audio or video tape recording. This recording can be followed up by the use of questionnaires, interviews (as in the IPR studies of Elliott (1983) and Rennie (1990), or by the use observational rating scales carried out by a non-participant. All these methods are accessible to practitioners, provided their theoretical orientation and the context in which they work allows them to record sessions. There are still contexts where any form of electronic recording is forbidden as damaging to the therapy. Theoretical arguments regarding the deleterious effect of recording on clients (Casement, personal communication), and on the therapeutic work, can be used by practitioners to protect their own fears of being seen in their practice context. It has been the observation of Jenifer that even the most senior practitioners embarking on a piece of doctoral research display this fear of making their work public and available to outsider observation.

Practitioner research

The tragedy of this ever widening split between research findings and practitioner interest is that most therapists still do not admit the need to design their own carefully crafted research strategies to help them understand better their work with their clients. Research into psychotherapy is taking place. Service providers are interested in wide-ranging evaluative studies which aim to discover and show efficacy in the form of the model of psychotherapy that they are funding. Academic departments in universities are traditionally interested in 'pure research' which demonstrates academic competence and supports theoretical advancement, rather than research as applied to practice (McLeod 1999: 6–8). All this has encouraged a division of labour between researchers and the researched practice context. In addition, research that is politically relevant or academically validated does not seem to answer the need of practitioners to understand their own practice based experience.

Here it may be useful to consider how psychotherapy research could be of real use to practitioners. What is necessary is the development of research methodologies which take into account the complexity of the context in which they work, and which honour the individuality and ethical requirements of therapists and their clients. McLeod (1999) has argued for the development of 'practitioner research in counselling' and, by implication, in psychotherapy, as a particular arena for research. He encourages practitioners to develop 'methodological pluralism', drawing from a wide range of established research methodologies. His ideas have been taken up with some enthusiasm in the United Kingdom, although the wide range of methodologies applicable to specific practitioner issues and research questions which McLeod reviews are rarely used in full. Psychotherapy practitioners who do venture into research projects, perhaps attracted by the possibility of gaining doctoral status, tend to be attracted solely to qualitative research and, in particular, heuristic and hermeneutic methodologies (Moustakis 1994; see McLeod 1999). The heuristic approach encourages qualitative researchers to immerse themselves in a real life situation, to reflect deeply upon this experience and then to arrive at their own hermeneutic or interpretative understanding. There is a danger that methodologies which make the researchers' personal reflections central can be used to validate these researchers' own assumptions while the ideal qualitative attitude of open inquiry into an observed phenomenon is sidelined. Here the methodologies developed through academic and evaluative models of research could still be made useful as a check on personal bias. This is commonly known as triangulation of methodologies. For instance, a qualitative inquiry carried out with a restricted number of participants could be followed up by a second line of inquiry in which a questionnaire based on the themes arising from this inquiry, as perceived by the practitioner researcher, could be administered. The third part might be to send questionnaires out to a much wider population and include measurable data sets.

A particularly useful research tool, which has been developed with individual practitioners in mind, is the Clinical Outcomes in Routine Evaluation (CORE) questionnaire. This is described succinctly by McLeod in his book, *Practitioner Research in Counselling*, (1999) itself an excellent guide for all therapists in any way interested in inquiring seriously into their own practice.

> The main element of the CORE system is a 34-item client-completed questionnaire, which is hand scorable, and gives scores in four main clinical domains: subjective well-being, symptoms, functioning, and risk/harm. There are also 18-item short forms of the questionnaire, which can be used weekly during therapy to monitor on-going change. Items are straightforward, easily understood statements, to which the client responds using a five-point scale.
>
> (McLeod 1999: 91)

The CORE system was launched in 1998 and is, at the time of writing, used almost exclusively by agencies, public health providers and institutions. Jenifer knows of only one practitioner colleague who regularly uses CORE in her own independent practice setting. This seems sad, particularly as the designers of CORE (Mellor-Clark and Barkham 1997) were particularly interested in developing a substantial data bank for all psychotherapy practitioners. Other useful and encouraging books for practitioners moving towards and interested in researching the outcomes of their own practice are McLeod's earlier publication, *Doing Counselling Research* (1994) and Parts 2 and 3 of *Evidence-Based Counselling and Psychological Therapies* by Rowland and Goss (2000). Less focused on methodology for practitioner researchers but interesting exemplars of psychotherapeutic approaches that have been subjected to some type of outcome research are *Outcomes of Psychoanalytic Treatment* by Leuzinger-Bohleber and Target (2002) and Wampold's *The Great Psychotherapy Debate* (2001).

All thoughtful practitioners go to supervision and there share their observations of the therapy *process* and *outcome* with specific clients or groups of clients and yet they do not see this as a possible useable research methodology. In optimal supervisory situations, *theories of change* are discussed, challenged and tested. Practitioners are made aware of variables pertaining to their own assumptions, and of patterns of relationship and their effect on the work with the client examined. New strategies of intervention are *designed and tested out*. In other words research orientated procedures are integral to good supervision. We suggest that by formalizing and refining this consultancy forum practitioners could develop their own body of published research into the process and outcomes of psychotherapy practice. Psychotherapy and counselling supervision itself has become the subject for research enquiries (Carroll 1996), but more in order to discover what are the supervisory tasks and what is effective supervision. How the supervision context can be used to encourage practitioners to research into their own effectiveness has not, at the time of writing, been developed. The focus of such an inquiry is likely to be on the *process* issues in psychotherapy practice rather than on the *outcomes*, although it can be argued that any refinement of methodology is in service of the end result.

It is still a puzzle to us why, in spite of a strong interest and involvement in psychotherapy research and inquiry, we notice our own personal reluctance to use almost any form of *structured* research methodology, process or outcome, or to evaluate the outcomes of our own session by session work with clients. Nor do we systematically link objectives to outcomes, although we do carry out regular 'reviews' with clients and could develop some sort of measure or structured record of this process. This lack of application could be dismissed, or excused, as due to a lack of time or energy, but we suspect there is a deeper reason linked to a hidden arrogance (or fear) regarding the approaches that we have, so far, developed in our own practice. This reluctance seems to be shared with most other practitioners, despite generous encouragement by some researchers to share and make user-friendly their methodologies. A particular example is the CORE questionnaire, described above, which has been made available for use by individual practitioners who are encouraged to use it for their own information or to send in data for general analysis and comparison. In addition, a qualitative discovery orientated approach, such as the hermeneutic methodology of Moustakis (1994), and aimed towards specific questions arising from the therapist's own practice, could be used. Such types of research avoid the usual critique of artificial non-applicable research, and could inform the theory of change being used by the therapist, and link it to the presence or absence of any progression from *objective* to *outcome*.

Personal example of the development of a qualitative research *attitude* to practice events (by Jenifer)

A question which regularly arises for me in my own practice is concerned with the level at which clients are using the insights gained in sessions regarding their inter-personal strategies in their home and work settings. I cannot follow my clients home, nor have I, so far, had the courage to ask them to tape-record their interactions with others outside the consulting room. However, occasionally a client will keep journal-type notes each week and bring these to the session to discuss. My early psychoanalytically orientated training for many years led me to resist reading these notes, believing that this would detract from the quality of the therapeutic relationship. My experience is that this refusal itself was often perceived as a withdrawal from contact on my part, and that only a few clients seemed to be hiding behind their written observations. So now with most clients I have experimented with giving full attention to these writings, willingly agreeing to keep them to read between sessions when asked to, and finding time to immerse myself in the valuable data offered so freely. I can often get first-hand information about the moment to moment quality of the social interactions engaged in by my clients. I also reflect upon the symbolic and hidden meanings in the material, and then check out my impressions regarding the underlying themes in these other relationships with the client, grounding our discussion in real life situations, including the interactions taking place between us in the consulting room. Together we can design an experimental shift of behaviour based on our understanding of the themes emerging from these discussions. Further journal notes by my client are likely to comment upon these experiments and my further immersion in the written material can initiate another cycle of exploration.

The Impossible Enterprise? workshop

Relevant here are the Impossible Enterprise? workshops mentioned earlier. These workshops began by discussing and comparing the definitions of the purposes and expected outcomes of therapy across the three main theoretical orientations: psychoanalytic, cognitive-behavioural and humanistic. Objectives were defined to participants as 'purposes, aims, goals, intentions, aspirations' while outcomes were defined as 'results, consequences, conclusions'. Participants were introduced to a comparison of the variance between researcher and practitioner (where these roles are carried out separately) in their approach to objectives and outcomes of the psychotherapeutic enterprise. See Table 4.1 for a summary of this distinction.

Table 4.1 Comparison of variance between researcher and practitioner

	Researcher seeks to ...	Practitioner seeks to ...
Objectives	Clearly articulate and specify Make measurable Generalize Quantify Audit	Facilitate initial aims Explore underlying aims Look beyond Revisit Reframe Relate to own objectives
Outcomes	Specify criteria for change Specify procedures (manualized therapy) Establish a range of measures Operationalize audit (questionnaires) Include third parties Link to clearly specified objectives	Check client experience and satisfaction Relate to own experience of outcomes Link to procedures used Reflect on process of change and growth Find out how much clients' initial aims have been achieved or revised Learn from feedback

The participants were then asked to complete a short questionnaire (see Figure 4.1), regarding their own views of the objectives and outcomes of psychological therapy, and invited to discuss these with another workshop participant before filling in their own answers. Participants were recommended to personalize their responses by keeping one particular client in mind while filling in the questionnaire.

QUESTIONS TO BE EXPLORED *EXPERIENTIALLY*

- What do participants in the therapy project expect?
- What does therapy achieve?
- Does therapy benefit individuals, families and communities?
- Does the therapist think they have made a difference?
- In what circumstances does therapy become ultimately harmful?

Figure 4.1 Questionnaire

The questionnaires were collected up and subjected to a thematic analysis. The first question, regarding expectations and aims, was most usually answered on behalf of the client rather than taking into account the therapist's aims as well. Client expectations most generally cited were for relief of pain and despair and to feel better, although wish for change and self-understanding also featured prominently. Many of those responding noted that these aims differed according to context, motivation and the level of personal responsibility taken by the client. Some clients were described as passively seeking some form of active intervention or advice from their therapist. Those participants of the workshop who included in their response the expectations of the therapist emphasized above all that their aim was for the client to achieve positive change through their experience and use of the therapeutic relationship. More pragmatically, contractual commitment to regular attendance and to working on themselves was also cited as part of the therapist's expectations of the client. The second question was answered in ways which matched this first question, with a continuing emphasis on insight in the form of expansion in awareness, understanding and acceptance of self, increased functionality, freedom of choice and greater ability to enter into authentic relationships. Less often cited was the solving of immediate problems or the relief of symptoms. Questions regarding the practitioners' views as to the overall level of beneficial or harmful effect of therapeutic activity to the client and their social context were answered more cautiously. Generally, there was agreement as to the probable beneficial effect of therapy dependent on the therapist's professional probity and ability to put aside personal issues and avoid any misuse of power. A full analysis is laid out in Table 4.2 (italicized data indicates recurring answers).

Table 4.2 Practitioners' views of objectives and outcomes

Questions (to be explored experientially)	Answers
What do participants in the therapy project expect?	Client: *Support and safety; change; self-understanding [insight]; feel better [despair and pain less]*; help, *solutions*, advice; symptom relief *[cure]*; specific outcome; learning about the world; to talk; expansion; *authenticity [depends on context, motivation, owning of problem]* Therapist: *[fewer answers] positive change through the experience of therapeutic relationship;* emotional work from client; regular attendance and time/money invested; mutual authenticity; challenge; containing client's feelings
What does therapy achieve?	*Increased insight, self-awareness, acceptance and understanding; more freedom of choice;* new opportunities; meaningful relationships; *ability to talk, be heard and express emotions securely; able to own and accept problems; behaviour change;* improved life quality and self-worth; *containment;* less maladaptive strategies; *hope*
Does therapy benefit individuals, families and communities?	*Can do so but also can create conflicts and challenges* when difficult family and social dynamics; only when culture and context is fully taken into consideration; *if increased communication;* depends on external motivation and engagement; initial tension but ultimate benefit possible; dependant on practitioner's qualities.
Does the therapist think they have made a difference?	*Usually beneficial*, at least as far as individual's experience of *therapeutic relationship* is concerned; if client collaborates; *to some degree*; if client continues process; *depends on client's subjective view*; can be negative; if feedback positive.

Questions (to be explored experientially)	Answers
In what circumstances does therapy become ultimately harmful?	*Therapist's own unconscious unresolved issues; misuse of therapist power for own ends; lack of boundaries;* therapist assumptions and projections; over-emphasis on long therapeutic relationship; over-use of interpretations; mental state of client de-stabilized; other relationships destroyed; client made *over-dependent* on therapist; lack of supervision, internal and external; lack of competence; clients own experiential flow not considered; mismatch; premature ending; insensitive therapist; *collusion*; not enough resources

So far, what has been learned from these workshops with psychotherapy practitioners is that those who take part are generally knowledgeable and confident about the objectives held by themselves and by their clients and are generally optimistic about the likely outcomes. This is, of course, an example of a qualitative inquiry within a very small population and needs to be balanced by a similar inquiry into the opinions of clients of psychotherapy. This could be achieved more easily within a group of psychotherapy trainees who are involved in their own personal therapy, but this would in our view be too particular a group of individuals. To access clients in an agency setting may be possible, although it is potentially difficult given that the agency would have to be convinced as to the usefulness of this inquiry to their own project. To access individual clients seen in private practice would be even more difficult and would involve the cooperation of their therapists. The development of a particular type of 'practice research network' (PRN) as described by Zarin et al. (1996, cited in Barkham and Mellor-Clark 2000) might make this endeavour more possible. A practice research network involves 'a large number of clinicians who agree to collaborate to collect and report data' (Zarin et al. 1996, cited in Barkham and Mellor-Clark 2000: 147) in their usual practice settings and then to pool this data and subject it to analysis. Up to now PRN research has taken place in the United States, among members of the research group of the International Association for Counselling (IAC) and in contexts where academic research experts are available to investigate the data obtained. Once again, individual practitioners need to be more actively motivated to explore their own practice in an open-minded fashion, risking discoveries about the *outcomes* experienced by their clients and questioning the *objectives* of their own psychotherapy enterprise.

Concluding response

Gabrielle

Like Jenifer, I am interested and surprised that I, along with all the practitioners I know in private practice, conduct no research, relying on my own observations of clients' behaviour, appearance, changed relationship with me both to decide that the therapy has reached a conclusion and that the outcome was satisfactory. As I reflect on this, it seems very dangerous and arrogant not to challenge myself to assess whether my way of working does result in clients' objectives being achieved. I have the basis of research because I also review informally, with clients, their progress, assessing with them which objectives have been achieved and any new objectives that have arisen. However, I have not looked on this as research or as having the potential to be a research project. I have considered that the main purpose of research is to counter attacks, as I perceive them, from the medical profession who are frequently immensely sceptical of talking cures. Thus I have thought that research had to be of sufficient rigour to counter the opposition and therefore had to be done by academics onto whom I have projected considerable power, compared to myself as a private practitioner.

Needless to say I have been aware that some clients do not feel helped by me and, even when there has been an agreement, following a review, that the objectives have been met and an ending is appropriate, I have remained doubtful as to whether therapy has made any difference to their lives. Rather than ask these people for feedback, I have hoped that I was wrong and that they had remained in therapy because it had been helpful, even if I could see no resulting changes in them. While this might have been the case, these clients may also have continued because they always hoped something would change or because I had induced a dependency that was not being resolved owing to my inability to find a method of working that would have done so. I think this head-in-the-sand approach was probably due to a fear that my belief in the power of therapy would prove to be wrong and I have therefore wasted a lot of training and time.

While not challenging myself about outcome research, I have been interested in practitioner research. For the past ten years BACP has had annual research conferences and since 2001 has published a research journal, the *CPR* (*Counselling and Psychotherapy Research*). I have attended these conferences and read the journal and found some of the research very challenging on some occasions and encouraging in others. I have found it challenging when it has been clear that my method of working needs to be changed and encouraging when something I do has been confirmed as useful. An example is a piece of research by Hanson (2004) which showed that self-disclosure, carefully planned and done skilfully was helpful to clients. (This, however, suggests I am able to use research which practically helps me but I am unwilling to challenge myself!)

In common with many psychodynamic therapists I have always been concerned that I do not introduce anything into the therapy that asks clients to do something for me, such as completing a questionnaire or permitting me to make a recording. The reason for this is that the act of doing something for me may well lead a client to wonder whether their response will please, displease or have no effect on me. For this reason questionnaires during the therapy are not used by me or by many other psychodynamic-psychoanalytic practitioners. For similar reasons I also feel considerable resistance to introducing sound or video recording to sessions. Even if the recording is done from the very first session, the act of asking clients' permission to record our sessions requires them to give or refuse permission. In doing this, I believe that clients are being asked to do something for the therapist which immediately sets up an additional dynamic to the therapeutic relationship. Another reason why I have concerns about recording is that even if clients have been given all the information they need, and think they will be unaffected by the presence of a recorder, they may find that its presence has considerable impact on them. Informed consent cannot be given in advance without really knowing what the experience will be like. One can only be wise after an event, because only then does one have all the information (Syme 2003).

I have known people who were deeply disturbed by the presence of the recorder; disturbed to such an extent that the level of their voice changed pitch and they found it almost impossible to speak. Clearly the dynamics of the therapeutic relationship is altered by such an emotional response. While some might argue that this level of distress can be used therapeutically, and that clients do get used to the recorder so that they become unaware of it, others argue that therapists have no right to cause such disturbance. If therapists of a particular modality have cogent objections to the presence of recorders or the use of questionnaires then they must search for other means of assessing and evaluating work. The suggestion by Jenifer that supervision might be used as a research tool needs to be developed or other methods devised.

Little attention has been given to the dual relationship created when practitioners use their clients for research (Syme 2003). I have already mentioned the difficulty for a client in deciding whether to agree to sessions being recorded. There are similar difficulties for clients when being asked whether they will take part in some research. They may fear that if they refuse they will receive substandard therapy or be punished in some way. While this behaviour by a therapist would be unethical there is no reason why someone, who has perhaps been abused by people in authority, will know that therapists are different. McLeod (1999) suggests that an additional safeguard for clients and therapist/ researchers is to have an independent arbiter who can be contacted if clients feel under pressure to partake in research. Another difficulty for a therapist/researcher is that some clients try to second-guess the required outcome of the research and therefore give answers designed to please or to sabotage the work. This clearly depends on their relationship with their therapist. This possible bias cannot be prevented but should be acknowledged as a possible variable in any study. Therapists conducting research using their own clients can also be prone to bias because they want their hypothesis to be proved. This can be avoided by ensuring the data is analysed by someone who is impartial. I believe that it is probably better to conduct research on other people's clients who are found by advertising, rather than to use one's own clients.

Ex-clients are also used for research to acquire follow-up data about whether an outcome has been sustained. All the difficulties of how to reply to such a request may well be there, and some ex-clients may feel drawn back into the therapeutic relationship. It is probably wiser to use posted questionnaires when doing research with one's own ex-clients rather than face to face interviews; and if interviews are necessary, to use ex-clients of other therapists.

Despite the difficulties in avoiding dual relationships and not putting pressure on clients, I have no doubt that all practitioners need to maintain an enquiring mind and to test their hypotheses throughout the therapeutic relationship. This is a form of research where the practitioner has to have an attitude of a researcher. The profession needs to find a method of encouraging this research attitude, perhaps by turning it into a necessary requirement of the continuing professional development now asked of all practitioners. In this way practitioners could extend research from projects done for a master's degree or a doctorate to a normal part of everyday practice. Even more hopefully, perhaps practitioners might be inspired to creatively question their assumptions regarding their clients throughout the therapeutic encounter, beginning with the first session.

CHAPTER 5

Assessments and intakes in relationship to outcomes

Introduction

In this chapter, we explore the links between assessment and outcome in more depth. Assessment and outcome can be thought about as two ends of a circular journey in that, with experience, clues as to the probable results of a particular therapeutic encounter can often be apparent at the first session. Jenifer has had a longstanding interest in first sessions in psychotherapy practice. Her earliest research project focused upon how this first encounter between therapist and client influenced the process and outcome of the therapy sessions and included a questionnaire as to what information was sought by the therapist as part of the assessment process. Such research carried out now would need a combination of a widely distributed, questionnaire based survey with intense qualitative interviewing of key representatives working in different contexts and from a variety of orientations. In addition, information would need to be obtained from a wide range of clients: both those who have finished therapy for the time being and those still experiencing therapy or counselling. Significant would be the discoveries of Talmon (1990) regarding the efficacy of 'single session therapy'; and the reflections on the importance and immanence of the common curative factors in shaping the therapeutic relationship as offered by a host of writers, including Goldfried (1980), Bohart and Tallman (1999), Bohart (2000) and Wampold (2001). Questions would need to be asked as to how motivation, as expressed at the outset of therapy, influenced the process throughout. How can clients' own aims and motives be made central and how can clients be facilitated to state these openly and explore them thoroughly? These questions need to be explored without theoretical bias so as to discover more about how assessments influence the progress of practice, rather than to arrive at any rigid conclusions as to how assessments should be conducted. It is in this spirit, and with these questions, that we hope to explore the subject of assessment or, our preferred word, *intake*, in relation to the objectives and outcomes of psychological therapy.

What brings a person to psychological therapy?

Almost all clients come into therapy with life problems, even if these are hidden behind abstract or vague feelings of discomfort, which are not clearly manifested in their everyday lives. These problems are usually experienced overtly in the client's social interactions, causing distress and discomfort to them and to those around them. More rarely, clients bring their own inner feelings of dissatisfaction with their experience of their lives, even though they appear to others to be functional and successful. In either case, this may be a temporary state of disturbance or a recurring, chronic condition. The general objective for almost all clients, stated or otherwise, is to change their life experience, at least to some small extent, and to live in a more contented, harmonious way. Sometimes a wish to understand themselves better is expressed and this aim is usually more achievable from the practitioner's point of view.

Whether to use diagnosis

Professional practitioners, whatever their orientation and no matter how much they wish to avoid pigeon-holing any particular individual in distress, have to find some framework by which to understand their prospective clients. In medical settings, formal diagnostic categories are generally used, derived from the latest edition of either the *Diagnostic and Statistical Manual of Mental Disorders* (DSM, American Psychiatric Association 1994) or from the mental health chapter in the *International Classification of Diseases* (ICD) handbook. These classifications are framed in a language that assumes a medical model and which describes psychological distress as a form of disease manifesting in symptoms indicating the presence of mental disorder. Diagnostic labels are fundamental to the established medical approach to illness, which is to discover what illness is being suffered by a patient so as to offer the appropriate cure, remedy or treatment.

Psychological therapists vary considerably in their use of these medically based diagnostic categories. Those working in psychiatric settings need to use a common language with their medically qualified colleagues and are often required to provide a differential or multi-axial *DSM* diagnosis. Psychotherapy training often includes modules on medical diagnostic terms and psychiatric concepts. Reference to the different types of classified personality disorders, especially Borderline Personality Disorder, is very common in discussions between psychotherapists. More conventional psychotherapy researchers often use these widely accepted diagnostic categories to specify the focus of their enquiry. At the other end of the continuum are humanistic therapists and counsellors who are philosophically opposed to the use of any form of label in the description of a unique individual's experience of their particular human situation and state of mind at any one time and in any one place (Strawbridge 2001). Between these two points of view, there is a range of attitudes among practitioners towards the use of diagnostic terms and labels as part of the assessment process. What is often promoted is a flexible attitude that allows for a diagnostic label to be used as a tentative and temporary descriptive term, which brings with it a wealth of experience gained by practitioners working with other people who manifest similar types of psychological distress or disturbance.

In any case, rare is the practitioner of psychological therapy who does not use some system of categorization, especially in informal conversations with fellow practitioners or in supervision. It is interesting to speculate about how this process of classification might limit the aims and goals of both client and practitioner. People formally diagnosed with a 'personality disorder' are, in some contexts, deemed unsuitable for psychotherapy. Clients might present a practitioner in private practice with the diagnosis they have been given by a psychiatrist, thus pre-empting the assessment process and limiting the possible outcome towards which they might aspire.

The circular journey from assessment to outcome becomes a closed loop.

Clients and the problems they present

In the classic and ever-helpful book on effective psychological therapy, *Persuasion and Healing* (Frank and Frank 1991), five categories of 'those who receive or should receive psychotherapy' are described by the problems they bring to therapy. The categories are 'the psychotic, the neurotic or persistently disturbed, the shaken, the misbehaving and the discontented' (Frank and Frank 1991: 11). These descriptions are, in the Franks' view, more meaningful and descriptive than any purely medical diagnostic categories based on symptoms observed by professionals and not on a client's own experience. For many humanistic practitioners, the use of the words psychotic and neurotic are still too redolent of psychiatric terminology. Perhaps it is better to understand neurosis as a repetitive and fixed pattern of distressful reactions and psychosis as the experience of being out of touch with consensual reality. With these under-standings, the Franks' categories are a useful way to differentiate between prospective clients at an initial encounter.

Clients with a psychotic diagnosis bring into therapy their difficulties with their perceptions of a non-consensual reality, which are usually frightening and disturbing both to themselves and to those around them. Often they are on medication that distances them from the delusions they experience but which has its own unpleasant physical side effects. They are usually, in the Franks' terms, severely 'demoralized' (Frank and Frank 1991: 34–9), with low self-esteem, powerless and unable to cope. Psychotherapy can offer them supportive understanding of their inner world and coping skills, leading to better negotiations with their social world. This can involve straightforward information about accepted norms of behaviour, particularly useful to those who have been, to some extent, institutionalized by being psychiatric in-patients. Any assessment process needs to take into account the level of stigma and shame that has often been experienced by these clients and ensure a clear agreement as to the purpose of psychological therapy and the use that they can make of it. Although most people experience somewhat psychotic fantasies from time to time, such is the societal fear of any form of psychosis that great care has to be taken to ensure that the objective of therapy serves the client's need rather than an external demand for social adjustment. For example, people with paranoid tendencies can learn how to accept and understand their reactions and to use therapy to check out the reality of their more alarming fantasies:

Brian put down the phone angrily. His girlfriend seemed to be so disloyal and, yes, even dangerous. She had discussed him with her friends and made jokes about their recent quarrel. Perhaps she had already called his doctor and his stepmother, who would be calling the psychiatrist even now. Soon he would be back in the psychiatric ward, his medication increased, unable to read or work on his computer. He turned despairingly towards his desk, covered with pages from his PhD thesis. His eyes fell upon a card pinned up above the printer, with the words, in his own careful calligraphy, 'You can always talk it through . . .' He remembered the promise he had made to Anne, his therapist: to find somebody with whom to check out his worst fears before running with them. He still had some sessions booked in with her, as needed. He could even telephone her, and see if she agreed with him about this being the end of his hope of a normal life. She would take him seriously.

Neurotic clients probably form the majority of those who use psychotherapeutic help on a regular basis. This is because they are categorized by their experience of a persistent recurrence of distressing symptoms in the form of depression and/or anxiety, with regard to their self-image, their physical health, their careers and their ability to cope with personal relationships. These feelings can, when severe, lead to withdrawal from social contact, self-destructive behaviours and overwhelming despair. Although medication is continually being developed and refined in an attempt to alleviate and suppress these disorders, the root cause of neurotic disturbance can usually be traced to a fixed attitude towards themselves and others. These are typically established in childhood and are now no longer a necessary *strategy for survival,* but one which leads to repeating, dysfunctional patterns of thought, feeling and action. These clients can be helped towards a more harmonious social existence if the psychotherapeutic alliance can be used to understand and then to challenge this belief system, through encouraging clients to experiment with different insights, more realistic emotional states and new behaviours. However, the original assumptions on which the strategies for survival were based are usually held rigidly, maintained by the client's present social system and difficult to give up. Neurotic clients may need to return to some form of therapeutic help several times, when their life situation induces the old repetitive response. An evolving process of assessment is more likely to succeed if a constructive working alliance is established which encourages understanding of these survival strategies, their roots in the past and their activation of the present destructive patterns of reaction. Objectives can then move from insight through emotional expression to active behavioural experiments. Outcomes are likely to be provisional, unfolding and expanding over time:

Rebecca took her brand new chequebook with her to the session. She felt an odd mixture of pride, guilt and terror as she made out the cheque, signed it shakily and handed it to her therapist. She was still reeling from her experience of the last few weeks, which had seemed to consist solely of confrontations, real or imagined, with her mother. She had finally insisted on them having separate bank accounts and on paying only a proportion of her monthly pay into her mother's account. The years of asking her mother for permission every time she used their joint account seemed to be over. She could feel relieved, her therapist suggested, or she could follow her old pattern of self-blame, castigating herself for being selfish, thoughtless and difficult. Hearing these familiar words in her therapist's calm, slightly humorous, tone of voice gave her some distance from them. She began to smile and then to giggle. How long would it be before she could grow up enough to forgive herself for taking care of herself and her needs?

Clients who have, in the Franks' (1991: 13) terminology, been 'psychologically shaken', by life events use psychotherapy or, more usually, some form of *counselling*, when faced with disturbing or traumatic life events with which they feel unable to cope. These situations are experienced as crises and can include recent bereavement, illness, accident, assault or perceived failure. The work of a therapist can initially be focused upon supportive understanding and normalization of the reactions being experienced, whether these are uncontrollable emotions, sleep disturbance, bizarre thoughts or self-denigration. Practitioners need to assess, with their clients, what assistance is needed at this time, and this may involve giving information about legal, medical or social resources. Above all, people in crisis need to be encouraged to remember their usual coping skills and support systems and to use them. Sometimes this work can be straightforward and very few sessions are needed for the client to return to their normal functioning. For some clients, however, the recent painful life event has triggered defensive and disruptive patterns established in response to previous traumatic experiences, especially those laid down as part of childhood learning. In these cases, work on neurotically fixed belief systems and repressed emotions may be needed before clients can return to their lives, with enhanced insight and emotional flexibility. These clients are initially motivated to seek help in achieving their objective of a return to normal functioning. This goal can be fully respected and validated, even though it is unlikely that any disruptive experience is likely to leave an individual, or a group of individuals, unchanged:

Jane worked in a bank and was present when the premises were raided and a colleague badly wounded. She didn't take time off work but began to find she couldn't concentrate at work or sleep because of recurrent images during the day of the hooded raider, and nightmares. She didn't feel herself and wanted to get back to normal. Her employer offered her counselling which she accepted somewhat reluctantly. In her first session with her counsellor, Tim, she was surprised at how easy it was to tell him what happened and found herself recalling the time when her parents' house was burgled. The suggestion by Tim that the feelings from the two seemingly different events might be related interested her and she agreed to come back and explore this further.

Clients who are perceived by others as 'misbehaving' (Frank and Frank 1991: 13) are usually *sent* to therapy by those who find their behaviour disturbing. This may be because they are demonstrating addiction, being aggressive or violent to others, disobeying their parents or superiors or, in some other way, not conforming with the established norms of their social context. They are sent to see a therapist because their behaviour is seen as having a psychological trigger rather than being purely due to a desire to be anti-social. For these clients, motivation to use therapy and to lead a different life is likely to be extremely low, except in those cases where there is enough despair about their life situation. One option for the practitioner is to enter into a non-judgemental, but also non-collusive, dialogue about the value system held by the client and its origins. These clients are, at best, 'visitors' (Elton Wilson 1996) to the therapeutic space, 'contemplating' (Prochaska and DiClemente 1986; Dryden 1991: 88–9) possible change, which has been imposed externally, through some sort of *counselling,* but without much hope. If the therapist is prepared to explore their level of motivation and explain the need for them to work for themselves rather than for others, then a useful dialogue can, sometimes, be initiated. More fundamental psychological change is likely to depend on renunciation of the disruptive conduct, at least temporarily. This in itself will make a difference to the client's life and may provide space for more active work on the underlying reasons for the damaging behaviour chosen by the client up to this time. Another change, very occasionally carried through, is the client's successful confrontation of the rules or standards being imposed by those who sent him or her to counselling. In these cases, the client is only 'misbehaving' in the eyes of the family, cultural or social system on which they have been dependent.

'Well, what a story I have for you this week!' exclaimed Mark, seemingly delighted to settle himself into his chair and lean forward, ready to embark upon yet more stories of the ongoing battle between his wife and his mother.

'Is it your own story this time?' asked the therapist, quickly, interrupting his flow. Mark sat back, offended. He did not want to talk about himself and his inner thoughts about his drinking habits and his use of the Internet to flirt outrageously and obscenely with 'pathetic' men seeking male partners. He was only coming to see this 'stupid' woman to get his wife off his back. Luckily his mother was paying for the sessions and it was a chance to take revenge upon them both by revealing all their weaknesses and faults. The therapist seemed to know that this was his motive for coming to see her, and was always asking him what fuelled his anger, what did he want from his life? These questions scared him.

The final type of client, described by the Franks (Frank and Frank 1991: 14) as 'discontented', is those who are inwardly dissatisfied with their life experience and whose external lives seem to be entirely functional. They often describe feelings of *alienation*, of feeling themselves as strangers and outsiders while apparently able to maintain personal relationships, bring up children and support themselves financially. They may have experienced therapy before, and even worked through traumatic experiences and difficult childhood experiences. Their concern is about the extent to which their lives are meaningful. These clients are probably best served by encouragement to face the universal existential issues, which face all human beings but which are usually avoided in the search for the comforting illusions of safety, of permanence and of community with others. Yalom (1980) has brilliantly summarized these issues as the four basic existential concerns – death, freedom, isolation and meaninglessness. Working through these existential anxieties to a place of responsibility, acceptance and personal choice can lead these clients to return to their lives with more ease, and often to some form of spiritual search. Of course, the therapy may also reveal these clients' unresolved, and somewhat neurotic, patterns of belief, which undermine their present life situations and which stem from early childhood experience. Insight into these hidden assumptions can relieve frustration and heal dissatisfaction at a more interactive level.

Janet was finding her first meeting with this therapist extremely uncomfortable. She had explained how much personal growth she had already accomplished through attending dream analysis workshops and the long-term women's group that she had started in the village. She had trained as a personal coach and was much in demand by her colleagues and friends as a mentor. Indeed it was one of these friends who had told her, in breathless terms, of the wisdom and insight of this man now sitting in front of her, and suggested that she and he would have so much in common. Her curiosity had brought her here for this session, which was proving to be useless. She had come to discuss her dissatisfaction with her marriage, but this man seemed unimpressed with her views about her husband's lack of spiritual energy. Instead, he was questioning the reasons behind her own feelings of despair and anger. In many ways this therapist reminded her of her husband, with his quiet insistence on the tragic elements of human life.

The therapist's use of assessment

For all these categories of client need, the key issue is an appropriate and thorough initial assessment session or, in some cases, a period of assessment. For each person, the practitioner has to put aside, temporarily, his or her own belief in the efficacy of psychological therapy in order to find out how to respond to the need of this client, at this time, in this context and with this particular problem. Ideally this means bracketing off theoretical concepts and meeting each person face to face, as freshly and as consciously as possible. At this time the question of what the client seeks to use therapy for, and what might be the outcome of that search, is the priority. Imposing one's own values regarding self-actualization, cognitive change, emotional release, embodied transformation or even basic problem solving is likely to obscure the client's own motivation. Nevertheless, most assessment sessions are, almost inevitably, heavily influenced by the therapist's own belief system and theoretical orientation.

There is some evidence that the psychotherapy profession is moving towards an integrated approach with regard to the provision of effective psychotherapy. Almost all trained and qualified therapists agree with the need for a strong working alliance, the facilitation of insight, a valid theoretical explanation and encouragement towards emotional expression and behaviour change. However, the language used to describe this therapeutic process and the manner in which it is carried out still differs considerably. For all therapists and counsellors, some form of intake procedure has to take place so that decisions can be made as to whether to continue with a contractual commitment. In Chapter 2, the influence of the therapist's theoretical orientation upon the objectives and outcomes of psychotherapy were discussed. In this section, we will explore in more detail the effect of the therapist's orientation upon the use made of an assessment period.

Generic assessment issues – what affects all intake sessions

First we need to summarize briefly what happens in almost all assessment sessions, whatever the orientation. The assessment process for all the psychological therapies, and for all practitioners, is used to decide whether a specific client is to be taken into a practice or an agency and offered a contractual commitment to joint work. To some extent, a core issue is the suitability of the prospective client for the type of counselling or psychotherapy provided in this context. This is particularly true for psychoanalytically orientated and behavioural psychotherapists, although the reasons given for this careful selection are somewhat different, as will be seen below. Humanistic and existential therapists are likely to hold less selective principles regarding intake sessions, maintaining their emphasis on inclusion rather than exclusion. Whatever their particular approach, the intake practitioner's intention is to make the initial assessment process welcoming and facilitative, while making clear that there are alternative possibilities and choices.

In almost all organizational contexts where counselling or psychotherapy is provided, printed information clearly explaining the professional practices of the service offered is often given to the client to read before the interview. Some private practice settings also offer leaflets describing the service offered. The leaflets can include information about the context, the nature of the counselling being offered, the qualifications of practitioners working there, the use made of the intake process, likely induction procedures, the extent of confidentiality offered, financial considerations and other pragmatic concerns. However, people in distress or impatient for help often do not read handouts and the following points need to be covered, preferably at the beginning of the intake interview:

1 Purpose of this assessment interview – to decide together whether psychological therapy is indicated as needed at this time
2 Length of time available for the interview

3 What the practitioner has to offer in qualifications and expertise
4 Issues regarding confidentiality and the limits of confidentiality
5 The practitioner's policy with regard to maintaining safety
6 General description of options likely to be offered at the end of the interview, including details regarding time available and financial matters

Whatever the theoretical orientation, in settings where there is a team of therapists, such as a counselling service or in a medical setting, the person who does the assessment does not necessarily become the ongoing therapist. This has to be made clear to the client straightaway both in any initial correspondence and phone calls and again in the assessment interview. It also means that the assessor has both to develop a rapport to help the client tell their story and to keep in mind their task, which is to give the allocation team a clear picture of the client, their needs and their objectives in seeking therapy so that they allocate a therapist appropriately.

These basic procedures of information giving and possible referral may in themselves affect the client's aims and intentions regarding the ways in which they can use therapy or counselling. Practical issues regarding finance and time available may arise, but more significantly clients may be disconcerted by the way in which confidentiality is to be handled, or by an emphasis on the need for disclosure in order to maintain safety. Many people turn to psychotherapy because they are holding some form of secret or sensitive information, or because they wish to express thoughts and feelings which they have kept to themselves in their external lives.

In some settings prospective clients are asked to complete a pre-assessment questionnaire. These questionnaires gather basic personal information such as the client's age, marital status and current family, family of origin, education, employment, presenting problem, past medical and psychiatric illness, details of current medication, previous suicide attempts. There is considerable disagreement between therapists on the use of such questionnaires (see Mace 1995). Some believe that use of the questionnaire improves attendance, provides the assessor with information and so prevents direct questioning which can be threatening and prepares clients for the assessment interview.

From the therapist's viewpoint the questionnaire can be important for research on objectives and outcomes and also for conducting an audit: this is a frequent requirement particularly for therapists working in the health service, further and higher education and agencies supplying psychotherapy. The contrary view is that questionnaires block the process of getting to know the client and in particular hearing the way clients tell their stories. Other objections to questionnaires are made. First, it is possible that the complexity of many questionnaires will put some people off and their subsequent non-attendance may be judged as lack of motivation, whereas it might simply reveal poor literacy. Second, some clients will not complete the questionnaire because of a fear that a number of people will read their responses and so compromise their confidentiality. Third, some clients become too upset by the questions to complete the questionnaire (Mace 1995).

Above all, the client will view their experience of the assessment interview as an example of the therapeutic approach on offer in this context, whether or not they are likely to work with this particular practitioner in future. Both participants will be acutely aware of the non-verbal communications underlying the overt dialogue, the questions and answers being explored. Trust building is an essential foundation for all intake sessions, although this can move from being desirable to presenting a potential difficulty if the prospective client has to be referred or refused at the end of the session. The personal characteristics of the practitioner may, of course, be influenced by the way in which they have been trained to carry out assessments and the theoretical concepts underlying their approach to this task. But whatever their backgrounds, most experienced therapists use the assessment session to:

- ascertain the client's reasons for seeking therapy (the presenting problems);
- explore their objectives;
- establish a rapport with the client;
- enable the client to feel understood;
- gather evidence of past and current psychiatric or medical illness;
- give the client hope and motivation so he or she wants to pursue the therapy;
- give the client the necessary information about practical arrangements.

In addition most practitioners try to ensure that the assessment is two-way, with clients also making assessments and asking questions. The client's main decisions are about whether they can entrust intimate information to the therapist, and whether that will be harmful; what benefits will result from a therapeutic relationship with the therapist; and whether they feel safe with the therapist.

Psychodynamic assessment

For psychodynamic practitioners, the assessment task is one of the most difficult tasks undertaken. Therapists attempt to use their empathic understanding to ascertain the nature of the client's predicament and discover the reasons for seeking therapy at that point in their life, and their objectives, at the same time they are trying to create sufficient distance to decide as dispassionately as possible on the likelihood of therapeutic success (Holmes 1995). This depends on the client being robust enough emotionally to manage a therapeutic process in which their view of themselves and the world can be explored in depth, and on the therapist being capable of giving a secure enough emotional environment in which change can take place. It is essential that the therapy does not leave clients more disturbed than when they started because the therapeutic work has been too invasive and unsettling.

Some psychodynamic practitioners make both a psycho-dynamic diagnosis, in which a client's strengths and weaknesses are listed and used to gauge the developmental level of their personality organization, and a diagnostic formulation, which endeavours to identify the core conflicts (Holmes 1995). For other practitioners this approach is 'too medical', but nonetheless they balance the client's objectives with therapeutic judgements about whether the work will involve regression to babyhood or childhood and whether in their judgement the client is emotionally strong enough to do this type of work. They are looking for evidence of how secure the early attachments were for the client and whether the current day problems could be linked with an insecure attachment. On the basis of such assessments the decision is made whether psychodynamic therapy is likely to be helpful or whether there are other approaches that are better suited to the person and their objectives.

Some therapists share their assessment of the core problems with a client. Others do not because of their belief that giving someone a diagnosis both labels and objectifies the client. These therapists share this belief with many humanistically oriented practitioners, especially person centred counsellors. Many psychodynamic therapists use their assessment formulation in supervision, revising it as they learn more about the client, and using it as a guide to keep a focus to the therapeutic work.

Psychodynamic practitioners consider the assessment, which may take one or more sessions, to be extremely important. Their assessment interview(s) has some specific functions in addition to the more generic assessment tasks listed above. The main ones are to:

1 Assess from the telling of the life-story:
   - the client's strengths and weaknesses, sometimes called the psychodynamic diagnosis (Holmes 1995);
   - the events from infancy and childhood which might have contributed to the client's current emotional distress;
   - the client's inner conflicts and defence mechanisms;
   - the central themes from the client's past and current life.
2 Give the client a taste of how a psychodynamic therapist works
3 Make a hypothesis of the client's core conflicts by bringing together the central themes of their past and current life

The method of acquiring the necessary life history and of attempting to understand the current predicament vary. The main aim is to gather the necessary information while empathically listening, with some therapists using a standard *proforma* to ensure that nothing is forgotten. The use of the pre-assessment questionnaire described above is often a particularly fraught issue for psychodynamic therapists. Although the questionnaire can provide useful information and leave the assessor free to use the assessment session to focus on the interview, the way in which the client tells their story in the room can be lost. The tone of voice when significant people are mentioned, the possible absence of reference to some significant people and the fluency with which the tale is told are all vital psychodynamic information (Holmes 1995).

Judgements may need to be made regarding core conflicts, levels of insecurity in attachment and in personality development, in order to assess how the client's childhood experience could affect the therapeutic alliance. If, for instance, they recount hospitalization of themselves as a baby or of their mother, this could lead the therapist to look at the way they tell their life history for evidence of insecurity and feelings of lack of worth and of never having felt loved. They might be looking for evidence of difficulty in sustaining relationships. They will be assessing how they felt with the client (therapist's counter-transference). If they felt unaccountably angry when with this client, this might indicate projected anger. Another consideration is whether some people in their lives are vilified and others idealized, in order to give a sense of how likely they are to sustain multifaceted relationships.

Some psychodynamic practitioners use structured interviews as part of the assessment process to assist in locating the emotional problem. For instance the adult attachment interview (George et al. 1985) was developed as a research tool but is used by some psychodynamic practitioners to assess the attachment status of adults. The purpose of this is to assist in the focusing of the therapy to enable the client to reach their objective. Whatever the client's surface goal, the psychodynamic practitioner's focus is likely to be upon the client's patterns of thought, feeling and behaviour, the origin of these patterns and their repetition within the therapeutic relationship. The particular purpose of assessment is to ascertain whether the client will be able to use beneficially a contained space in which to explore these matters, and to use the transference to heal the past, to understand the present problematic issues and to work through to a more realistic and productive way of life.

Existential–humanistic assessment

Philosophically, humanistic and existential theories can be said to maintain that every individual seeks to make their life meaningful through some form of self-actualization. This universal human tendency is described eloquently by Rogers (1967: 35):

> Whether one calls it a growth tendency, a drive toward self-actualisation, or a forward-moving directional tendency, it is the mainspring of life and is, in the last analysis, the tendency upon which all psychotherapy depends ... it is my belief that

it exists in every individual and awaits only the proper conditions to be released and expressed

To some extent then, every prospective client might be assumed to be motivated and ready to use fruitfully the facilitative conditions offered by a truly therapeutic relationship. Holding this assumption, many convinced humanists question the need for any form of structured or selective assessment process. In addition, person centred therapists are likely to eschew closed questions regarding the client's presenting problems and their hopes regarding the outcome of therapy. Mearns and Cooper (2005) warn against practitioners having their own 'agenda' regarding aims and goals for their clients. They may wish to understand their clients, to make their clients feel better or, particularly in the case of trainees, to demonstrate their competence through achieving a beneficial outcome. Practitioners are encouraged to become aware of these, sometimes implicit, desires, to put them consciously aside, so as to facilitate the 'meeting at relational depth', which is fundamentally necessary for the client's journey towards self-actualization.

In practice, however, most existential-humanistic therapists carry out some form of assessment, with considerable emphasis upon this being a mutual two-way process based on, 'meeting existentially person to person' and 'establishing consensus about the client's needs and aims' (Mackewn 1997: 33). Mackewn also describes 'awareness and specific goals' as 'two poles of a continuum'. An increase in self-knowledge and subsequent self-actualization through the development of authenticity, presence and awareness is likely to be the outcome hoped for by most humanistic practitioners. The client is encouraged to take responsibility for their choices in life, including the decision to undertake psychotherapy or counselling. Respect for the client's unique needs is usually promoted. Humanistic therapists try to avoid information gathering through the use of direct questioning and diagnostic thinking. Realistically, however, most gestalt, transactional analysis and modern person centred therapists realize the need to ascertain the particular personality features and possible problematic issues which could influence a proposed therapeutic engagement. Ongoing change, flexibility and expansion are accepted as part of all therapeutic journeys and a process of revisiting and reviewing evolving aims and goals with an increasingly motivated client is promoted.

Cognitive-behavioural assessment

Cognitive-behavioural therapists approach the assessment of prospective clients in a similar way as they would approach a research project. Their initial aim is to make an accurate formulation of the therapeutic task ahead and to do this they need to follow through the following steps:

1 *Elicit data*: The acquisition of as much 'critical detailed information as possible' (Hazler 2001) is vital to accurate formulation. The prospective client is asked in detail about their cognitive processes and belief systems as part of an in-depth enquiry into how these patterns of thinking, or 'schemas', link with unwanted emotional arousal and problematic behaviours. The focus is upon how the problematic issues are reinforced by present life events and environmental influence rather than upon causes based on early childhood developmental issues.

2 *Check motivation and availability*: Clients embarking upon cognitive behavioural therapy must be willing to undertake structured tasks within the therapy session and to carry out experiments in the form of 'homework' outside the therapeutic space. This means that selection for suitability is an accepted part of cognitive behavioural assessment.

3 *Establish clear and specific goals*: Together client and therapist explore the aims and objectives of the client, specifying as exactly as possible what outcome is sought and agreeing together about what cognitive changes and behavioural experiments might be needed to arrive at this goal.

4 *Make sure of a working alliance*: Beck describes the importance of 'collaborative empiricism' to describe how the client and therapist should ideally 'work together to test the validity of various hypotheses about the client's self and environment' (Hazler 2001). Unlike humanistic therapy, this collaborative relationship is not seen as a healing factor in itself but a necessary component of the work towards beneficial change.

These clearly defined assessment processes are intended to lead to a therapeutic engagement in which the therapist is likely, in the early stages of therapy, to be active and directive in educating the client into increasing levels of cognitive transformation and behavioural experiments. The use of diagnosis is accepted as an essential part of the formulation of a valid treatment plan. As therapy progresses, CBT practitioners move towards a more collaborative relationship with their clients, engaging in 'Socratic' debate and encouraging mutually designed experiments to promote behavioural, emotional and cognitive change. In order to work with clients who present with longstanding personality problems, cognitive behavioural assessment has recently broadened to include, when necessary, the identification of early maladaptive schemas (Young and Swift 1988; Linehan 1993) formed during childhood and resulting in the current presentation at assessment of problematic patterns of thought, feeling and behaviour. The similarity of this focus to the theory behind psychodynamic assessment procedures can be masked by the terminology used.

Integrative assessment

Supposedly, integrative psychotherapy practitioners should be able to take advantage of all the accumulated knowledge and wisdom regarding assessment, and to select the approach to assessment that fits their own integrative approach. Some integrative or eclectic approaches promote a multifaceted framework for assessment so as to ensure a comprehensive appraisal of the client's needs. This might entail the systematic use of a schedule of modalities such as Lazarus's (1981) 'BASIC ID', which ensures that each client's behaviour, affect, sensation, imagery, cognition, interpersonal (functioning) and (use of) drugs/biology are all taken into account before deciding how to treat an individual client. Alternatively, each client's psychological distress as manifested by their current presenting problems can be framed by the dynamics operating between the past 'back then', the present both 'out there' and 'in here' (Jacobs 1988) and the probable future (Elton Wilson 2000b; Lapworth et al. 2001). The cognitive analytic therapy (CAT) (Ryle 1990) approach to assessment is summarized below in the context of brief or time focused therapy. Any form of integrative therapy has to take into account contextual factors whether this be time available or societal influence. However, for increasing numbers of therapists moving towards an integrative approach the major perspective to be considered is likely to be the readiness of the client for therapy and their availability to make use of the common curative factors described below as 'change strategies' by Goldfried (2003):

• Mutual expectation that therapy will help
• Optimal therapeutic relationship
• Feedback given to client by an 'objective other'
• Focus on interactive processes
• Encouragement of corrective experiences and reality testing

In order to evaluate this potential, verbal questions and responses are less important than the interpersonal non-verbal communication taking place between practitioner and prospective client. Once again Bohart's (2000) reduction of the task of the therapist to ensuring 'engagement' and 'explanation' becomes relevant and encompasses the structured enquiries of the CBT practitioner as much as the relationship focused considerations of psychodynamic and humanistic therapists.

Brief therapy assessments

The assessment interview for brief or short-term therapy is likely to conform to the theoretical orientation of the assessing practitioner. For psychodynamic therapists there are often stringent selection criteria, such as 'sound basic personality', a history of 'satisfactory interpersonal relationships' and 'ability to cope with reality and to bear frustration and conflict' (Malan 1975: 21). These characteristics can be ascertained initially during the assessment. The reason for this is that working briefly often involves deliberate provocation of anxiety (Sifneos 1979), or focusing at as high an emotional level as possible on separation-individuation problems (Mann 1973). As with any other therapy, the psychodynamic therapist would be acting irresponsibly if they left a client more disturbed at the end of therapy than at the beginning.

Cognitive-behavioural therapists have specialized in time efficient therapeutic interventions and evaluate the prospective client with regard to the likelihood of their being able to take advantage of verbal debate, written material and homework tasks, all aimed towards clearly specified outcomes.

It could be argued that humanistic and existential therapists are philosophically opposed to any form of brief therapy in that any limitation of time can be seen as a therapist imposed condition and so limiting 'unconditional positive regard from the therapist and ... the natural growth processes inherent in clients' (Elton Wilson 2000b: 254). They do, however, often have to work in settings where brief therapy is all that can be offered.

The inescapability of finite time is itself an integrative factor influencing all orientations and approaches, as the demand for more economy of time and resources has infiltrated psychotherapy provision. Practitioners have needed to examine the essential elements of their practice, their own theoretical belief systems and their methodologies. One specific integrative approach has been crafted from this requirement for brief therapy. Ryle's (1990) cognitive analytic model of integrative therapy offers assessment in the form of a shared process of enquiry leading to a mutually agreed understanding of the current problematic patterns and their roots in the past. From the expertise and theoretical rigour of the behaviourist, the practitioner offers an empathic, here and now assessment of the client's present concerns as well as exploring with a psychodynamic lens the personal history from which they arise. In addition, the practitioner explores the immediate needs of their clients and their readiness for a time limited encounter with psychological therapy. The aim of the CAT practitioner is to establish collaboration between client and therapist and to share their thinking openly with clients, offering 'reformulations' and 'goodbye letters' to be jointly designed. Out of this assessment a time focused contractual commitment can be designed, with opportunities for collaboration, discussion and mutual review. Essential to this process are the relationship skills of the humanistic practitioner as well as the psychoanalytical therapist's sensitive ability to discern transference issues, and to develop an enduring working alliance.

Ryle (1990) evolved his particular approach in response to the needs of psychiatric patients, often severely disturbed and known as 'revolving door' patients because of their repetitive constant cycle of crisis, therapeutic provision followed by dropping out. This approach eschews the stringent selection criteria often recommended for brief therapy assessments.

There are an increasing number of contexts in which brief therapy is the standard form of therapy provided including employment assistance programmes (EAPs), many primary care settings, student counselling services and some voluntary agencies. To some extent selection operates in the assessment for these services, but the difficulty in finding suitable and immediate therapeutic provision for their clients puts pressure on the person carrying out the intake interview to provisionally accept a client for a brief therapy contract. The need to respond to a client's current needs can encourage the development of a form of assessment more focused upon the client's immediate needs at this stage of their life. The therapist can be encouraged to accept that for clients, in Talmon's (1990: 134–5) terms, 'therapy starts before the first session and will continue long after it'.

Concluding remarks

Jenifer
I am aware that the link between making assessments and making contractual commitments has not featured much in this chapter so far. I wonder whether the difference between theoretical orientations and contexts affects the importance of making a clear contract? Do we need to say any more about this?

Gabrielle
Yes, we do. Some therapists are very unhappy with the whole concept of a contract: perhaps because contracts are so much part of the modern capitalist world with targets, audit trails and consumers' charters. Sills (1997) points out there are three types of contracts; the administrative, the professional and the psychological. The purely administrative contract, concerning cancellation policy, frequency and location, is considered important because many clients who make formal complaints about their therapist are doing so because this has not been honoured. Fear of complaints is not a reason to abandon contracts but rather to ensure they actually reflect one's practice. From the point of view of objectives the professional contract is very significant. It is about the overlapping issues of the areas of concern that are to be explored, the focus of the work, the agreed purpose and the goals. The question is whether it has to be outlined to a client or whether it is only carried in the therapist's head.

Some theoretical orientations and approaches to therapy do make explicit professional contracts: examples are CBT and brief psychodynamic therapy. And in some particular contexts the professional aspect of a contract is always made clear, again often associated with the brevity of the work. Some agencies with a specific focus do not make a professional contract because the agency assists people with a particular problem such as bereavement or rape. It is therefore implicit that such events are the reason and the focus of the work.

Personally, I am aware that I do not make a professional contract in any formal and spoken way, though, of course, I do carry in my head the reasons the client came and their hoped for outcome, and I use diagnostic terms in supervision. The explanation may be that I do not routinely review the work; rather I review when either clients state they are stuck or I feel that we are having difficulties.

Jenifer

All you say about contracts is of interest to me, and I find it somewhat surprising. In my own practice, I probably emphasize the professional contract almost more than the administrative contract. I tend to be flexible about administrative details but to return regularly to the aims and goals in the form of regular reviews of the contractual commitment between my clients and myself. I usually initiate these reviews, not just when I am stuck, but at regular intervals, since I believe that almost all objectives change and transform over time. The longer the therapy, the more important these regular reviews seem to be. As long as they are not presented as tests of the client or of the therapy, but as explorations of where we are going and whether the therapy has been useful so far, it seems to deepen the commitment between my clients and myself. As a supervisor, I regularly suggest the use of reviews and clarifying the contractual commitment. However, I realize that attention to changing objectives does not always need to be verbally acknowledged and recorded to establish a professional level of commitment and to ensure continuing motivation.

Gabrielle

We have not really looked at how client's aims and motives are made central to the assessment, or at how hidden motives may undermine the therapy unless they are identified and addressed in the assessment. For instance a client's relationship with the referrer may have a significant positive or negative effect.

Jenifer
Again, in my own approach to therapy, the client's own aims and motives are central to the assessment process and indicative of their motivation. I learnt from transactional analysis (TA) the danger of not questioning aims that are broad, vague and unrealistic. Where possible, I try to move the agreed goals to a specific description, perhaps by asking, in TA fashion, 'How will you know when you are feeling better, have more self-confidence, understand yourself better, etc.?' More importantly, I increasingly understand good motivation as being the most important 'common factor' (Goldfried 1980; Bohart 2000) that leads to a reasonably satisfactory outcome.

I agree with you that hidden, and possibly detrimental, motives may need to be considered, particularly when the client seems to have been 'sent' to the assessment session rather than choosing to explore possible engagement in psychotherapy for themselves. In my own terminology, this is typical of the 'visitor' to the world of psychological therapy (Elton Wilson 1996) who is likely to need information about how therapy is conducted rather than any assumption that they are ready to engage. Of course this term could be used as a type of selective category alone, but my own view is that using the assessment session to 'visit' the therapeutic space is perfectly legitimate and useful to prospective clients.

Gabrielle
A contentious issue between therapists that we have discussed a little is the use of psychiatric labels. I rarely use them with a client because I think I am in danger of being patronizing by their use; but I would use them in supervision. I am aware of times when clients have been grateful for a referral to a psychiatrist and have found the diagnostic label useful. I have also found clients using a diagnostic label as a way of blocking the work. Perhaps my solution and that of other practitioners of not using labels is somewhat absolute.

Jenifer
Personally, I espouse the flexible attitude to the use of diagnostic labels, where they are used in a temporary and descriptive manner that takes account of the collective experience of other mental health practitioners. I am particularly wary of the effect of unrecognized and informal categories, such as the 'difficult' or

'fragile' client. For me these terms are even more likely to be stigmatizing and restrictive in practice. This discussion regarding diagnostic labels has highlighted the difference between 'intake' and 'assessment' in that the former allows the practitioner to prioritize openness and awareness towards each person attending for an intake interview. This means letting go of all assumptions and selective considerations, at least for a time.

Gabrielle and Jenifer
We have both become very aware in thinking about assessment in this chapter and linking it with earlier chapters that the non-verbal part of all assessments is critical. It has a parallel with the first sight the mother and the baby have of one another, which we now know from the neurobiologists (Schore 2003) is so important. The challenge for all therapists must be how to carry out the assessment in a rigorous way and yet reach out to the social essence of our clients.

CHAPTER 6

Outcomes: the ending

Introduction

Every therapeutic relationship, like every life, has a birth and a death, or like every journey, it has a beginning and an ending; these are marked by the assessment/intake and the outcome points. The end of a therapeutic relationship does not have to mean a complete ending, but rather, as the tarot death card symbolizes, it is a time for transition and transformation. Tibetan Buddhism describes the stages or 'bardos' between death and life, and maintains that each life contains a series of 'little deaths', experienced in the form of relationships ending, careers changing and homes being left (Sogyal Rimpoche 1992). These 'little deaths' or transitions are essential for maturation, because the successful negotiation of each transition results in personal growth.

Therapists are often more interested in the journey, but for clients the most important thing is likely to be the outcome and how it matches their objectives at the beginning of the journey. This book has focused on the objectives and outcomes, partly because it is from these that therapists have most to learn and also because they mirror in miniature the whole therapeutic endeavour.

In one sense each therapeutic relationship is unique and therefore no two outcomes or endings are identical, but one could still categorize them broadly into negative, and/or no change, or positive. It may be that the therapist and client could categorize the outcome differently. The important questions for therapists must be how the client perceives the outcome, whether it matches the therapist's assessment of the outcome and what can be learnt from this, and so used in another therapeutic relationship.

In this chapter we look at different types of outcomes in therapy. We share our own experience of the endings of therapeutic relationships, before moving on to discuss how outcomes are influenced by society, culture and politics. Finally we explore what we have learnt from writing this book together and any implications for psychotherapy generally.

Negative outcomes

Gabrielle
One way of defining a negative outcome is that something has gone wrong with the process of therapy and as a result the client feels damaged by the experience. This can be due to inexperience, incompetence or malpractice. Inexperience and/or incompetence can lead to poor assessment in which, for example, the therapist does not recognize the level of instability of a potential client, and instead of offering supportive therapy undertakes in-depth work, which destabilizes the client and causes a breakdown. Feelings of omnipotence on the part of the therapist can also lead to the view that they can help anyone. This is a very dangerous view especially when the breakdown of a client is always a possible outcome of such an attitude.

There are stages in a therapeutic journey when a client can feel considerably more depressed or more insecure and anxious. A skilled and experienced therapist knows this is a possibility and that for some clients this is so frightening that they are tempted to leave therapy prematurely. If they were to do this they would be worse than when they started therapy and the outcome would be negative. One way of avoiding this is for therapists to explain to clients early in the therapy that they may feel worse at some points while some very damaging experiences in earlier life are being explored and that it is important not to leave therapy at that point. The skill of the therapist is to offer a therapeutic holding while clients go through this work so that they stay and reap the benefit of the in-depth work.

It is not surprising that malpractice such as sexual, emotional or physical abuse of a client can result in a negative outcome. The effects of sexual abuse of a client are so stereotypical that they are described as the 'therapist–client sex syndrome' (Pope and Bouhoutos 1986, cited in Garrett 1994). Clients sexually abused by their therapists are much more likely to commit suicide, are more frequently hospitalized and show many other signs of disturbance.

When I think of my own work I am aware that there are occasions when I have not helped a client, which is a negative experience for them in the sense that their objective was not satisfied, even if subjectively they felt no worse. I am not aware of a client having become more disturbed from my misguided efforts. One cause of failure on my part is missing the level of disturbance in a client during the assessment and then not having the skills or experience to work with him or her. Another cause is not having sufficient empathy for a client's condition. I am now aware, as I mentioned in Chapter 1, that I am not able to help alcoholics because my life experience has left me frightened of them and therefore lacking empathy. I also think that once a week psychodynamic therapy is not effective with alcoholics. Also fear on the part of the therapist will always block therapy. This is one reason why it is important to ensure, as far as it is possible, the safety of the therapist when setting up a counselling practice or service (Syme 1994). A third reason for failure is when it seems to me that the 'chemistry', which is one catalyst for change, is not present between me and a client. This chemistry is hard to describe because it is felt at a deep level. It seems to be a two-way intuitive link, perhaps not unlike the bond between a mother and her child. When this link is present, it enables change. Yet another reason for failure is not having addressed issues, often due to my own blindness, which could have freed up the client had they been discussed. It has happened on a number of occasions that I have discovered something about myself in therapy or supervision and then I have heard it from the client. As mentioned in Chapter 1, it was only when I realized that feelings of envy were denied in my family and therefore by me, that I could hear clients' feelings of envy and help them to recognize it for themselves. It is fortunate when this happens before the client gives up. I am amazed at the way many clients hang on until their therapist 'wakes up' to an important issue.

I also am aware of clients who have rightly terminated work, almost as if they were aware that the therapist has gone as far as they can. I remember one client who worked with me for about 18 months at which point we finished by mutual agreement. I felt

I had gone as far as I could go and he felt stuck. He returned about a year later saying there were more issues he wanted to explore. This time we worked at much greater depth, partly because I was more experienced and could now 'hear' about sexual abuse and work with it, and partly because he was now ready to do that work. I was impressed by this man's wisdom and knowledge of himself.

Focusing on failures highlights for me the importance of good supervision and regular reviews. Both should enable one to look realistically and openly at what is happening in a therapeutic relationship, and enable the client to feel free to leave if the therapy is getting nowhere. Allowing a client to waste time and money on therapy that is going nowhere is indefensible.

Jenifer

What is a 'negative outcome' and who defines it as such? Gabrielle has explored some of the situations where the client feels damaged by therapy and where the therapist feels dissatisfied. However, the definition of a negative outcome may, to some extent, depend on the context and even on the orientation within which the therapy has taken place. For example if, during a period of therapy based in a GP surgery, a client continually visited their doctor with a series of anxious enquiries about what seem to be imagined physical symptoms, this would probably be seen by the doctor as being a negative outcome of the counselling carried out by the practice counsellor who would probably feel the same. This is a context, like many others, where there is a third party who takes an interest in any psychological change that might be taking place in the hope that it will show improvement of problematic behaviour. It is possible that the client has no interest in making this psychological change; thus the referrer's perception will be of a negative outcome and the client will achieve their desired outcome which is no change. This brings us back to the question of what an objective of therapy should be. Should the objective be that the client moves towards change in order to conform to the requirements of their family, their employers or the educational institute where they are studying? Or should it be that they alleviate their own personal suffering through therapy, regardless of the effect that might have on the people with whom they are interacting in their external lives, and who may even have directed them to therapy in the first place? In this case any continued psychological distress would mean there had been a negative outcome for the client, regardless of whether they had maintained their marriage, returned to work or passed their exams.

Another contextual element regarding the experience of a negative outcome is likely to be linked to a cultural mismatch in expectations regarding the purpose of therapy. My own searing memory is of providing therapy to a young Chinese woman student. On the surface, this client was highly Anglicized and had worked in a British business setting. The therapy seemed to be useful and she seemed eager to comply with my encouragement to experience her own needs and to expand her ways of being in the world, rather than fulfil the mysterious aims of her tutors, whatever these might be. However, no change occurred and we agreed to close down. At the last moment of the last session, she suddenly described herself as being, in my eyes, the 'client from hell'. Too late, I realized that she had brought to therapy the need, probably cultural, to conform, to obey and to avoid the shame of expressing personal needs.

From the therapist's point of view, a negative outcome is likely to be defined by the belief system underlying their work, influenced by their training and the theoretical orientation to which they are aligned. The cognitive behavioural practitioner is likely to presume failure where there is lack of evidence of any cognitive shift leading to behavioural change or to symptom alleviation. A humanistic therapist is likely to view as negative the continuing manifestation of an inauthentic false self which is reliant on conditions of worth, originally externally imposed. For a psychodynamic therapist, external change rapidly achieved through the therapeutic engagement is likely to seem superficial, a 'flight to health' and an avoidance of 'deep work' which might in itself lead to increased feelings of distress. An integrative therapist is more likely to fit their view of outcome, and of failed therapy to the client's own attitude, despite the particular theoretical concepts and methodologies dominating their particular approach to practice.

It seems that the degree to which outcomes are seen as negative may be dependant upon objectives hidden in the context where therapy is taking place **or** upon the views held by the therapist regarding the definition of a positive outcome. In any case a negative outcome is the opinion of the observer who makes such a judgement. Where a negative outcome is acted out and results in actual physical or psychological damage to the client or to any other person, there is usually unanimous agreement that this outcome is a negative one. Gabrielle describes above some of the self-damaging reactions of clients whose therapists have transgressed the boundaries regarding sex. Emotional abuse in the form of negligence, false promises or the encouragement of unsupported levels of dependency often form the substance of complaints made to professional associations by clients about their therapist. Direct emotional and physical abuse in the form of attacks upon the client's self-esteem or upon their physical self may take place but these are rarely described in the literature. Personally, I have experienced and witnessed some extreme interventions, which were perhaps intended to be therapeutic, but which led to 'shaming and blaming' or which actually could have led to physiological damage. I would include in this the couple's therapy workshop where the group leader instructed a husband to put a leash around his wife's neck and lead her round the room on all fours. I have witnessed ECT (electro-convulsive therapy) carried out on a frail elderly woman who left the room bruised and confused. I have heard humanistic therapists describe as emotionally abusive the manner in which Perls challenged Gloria in the famous filmed example of gestalt therapy (Shostrom 1965). But in this case Gloria herself commented that Perls had been the most helpful of all the therapists she had encountered. This shows how judgement of an outcome is dependent on 'the eye of the beholder'. However, probably it is the therapist's misuse and misunderstanding of the power they hold which contributes most powerfully to a train of events likely to lead to a negative outcome.

Perhaps it is important to remind ourselves of the centrality and complexity of the client's own readiness for the journey of personal work. Is the client seeking some alleviation from suffering, a state described by Frank and Frank (1991) as 'demoralization', so that he or she may become more functional in their daily lives? Are they seeking increased understanding of their problems so as to be able to tackle these with more autonomy and responsibility? Or is the client ready to take forward their increased understanding of their repetitive patterns so as to make experiments in life with different or expanded ways of thinking, feeling and behaving? Any concept of therapy as a staged process of recovery and transformation indicates constant movement, along with the principle that there is always more to be achieved. I endorse and repeat Gabrielle's strongly stated view that 'going nowhere is indefensible'.

Positive outcomes

Gabrielle
While thinking about this aspect I have talked to a number of friends who have had therapy. All were really interested in but unhappy about the concept of a 'positive outcome'. The preferred term was 'recovery', but not the sort of recovery following a physical illness or an operation such as an appendectomy where, given time, one is no longer aware of having been ill. This is well put by Fergusson (2004: 41–2) who had suffered a severe breakdown:

> What I now know is that the image of recovery to which I clung, with its longing for normality and ordinariness to return, is not possible in the way in which I had imagined, and indeed was a stumbling block along the way. Traumatic experience imprints itself, becomes part of what we are, and we live thereafter with a new knowledge of the depths and complexity within us. From this point forward recovery is not an end point, but rather our journey through life in its entirety ... It may even be helpful to view this journey as one around a spiral, in which each direction is equally important and will be taken in turn, as we move further outwards into the challenges of the wider world and then back into retreat within the centre of ourselves as we gain insight and come to know and accept ourselves with compassion.

The path to recovery from mental breakdown or severe loss involves transformation of feelings such as fear, anger and hate into an accepted part of oneself rather than a rejected part, and then their integration into oneself.

If our sense of negativity or guilt or failure is a deeply embedded part of our view of our place in the world then change will take place slowly. But when change does occur in even small ways it becomes possible to stop seeing ourselves as lost and hopeless, to begin to accept the whole of ourselves and to express ourselves with a measure of confidence. This is indeed transformation.

(Fergusson 2004: 41)

As I think of relationships with clients where I have been sure of their recovery I know that I have been involved in a relatively small part of their journey. They leave therapy having managed a difficult part of their life, with their destination reached for the moment, but this is also the starting point for moving on and the next part of their journey. This next part of the journey might be accompanied by friends and family, and at other times made with another therapist at a later point in their lives. Some clients make enormous changes in their lives, changing careers, leaving a relationship, exploring and accepting their sexual orientation, starting new and more satisfying relationships, but still a therapist is only there for a small part of the journey.

What have I seen and felt that has indicated recovery? This can be as small as a client becoming aware of my welfare and interested in me as a person after months of obsessive self-absorption. It can be that a client actually looks different. I assume that what one is seeing is tension resulting from fear and anxiety disappearing and thus changing the lines in someone's face. I can feel, and see that there is happiness. I can hear them telling me about the ways in which they handle life, themselves and relationships better. For some it is clear that they are more realistic about life, knowing that life is not easy and that ghastly things might happen to them and others, but that they will manage. Another sign of recovery is a client's capacity to think about themselves as an active agent in their own life and to be able to understand how they interact with other people. They realize that they do not always have to blame themselves and also that it is important to be gentle with themselves.

I never expect feedback from clients, but some keep in touch and years later provide some feedback that confirms that therapy made a huge difference to their lives and the effects were sustained. Some I never hear from again, but I do not forget them because I too have been changed by the work with them. Undoubtedly there are some clients with whom one has a much deeper relationship. I would go so far as to say that they are kindred spirits and that this aids the work. In another time and another place one might have been close friends, but the therapeutic relationship prohibits this. The question that remains for me is whether I can learn something from the therapeutic relationships in which there is clear recovery and use it in the relationships which do not work for the client. Or are there some relationships that will fail, not because of poor technique, but because change is not possible even when it is really desired by both parties?

Jenifer

I wonder whether the word 'recovery' is enough to cover the notion of a positive outcome. For me the word is related to some experience of retrieval, perhaps of a previous loss or, more positively, the revival of a previous positive state of mind. This seems to leave out the euphoria of a client who is released from patterns arising from strategies for survival formed in childhood and able to explore new and alternative ways of being in the world. The original strategies can remain as optional ways of responding to a situation but they are now subject to some choice as to their suitability. Nor is this expansion of choice limited to behaviour. It also applies to emotional responses and to ways of construing reality. Clients who are satisfied with their therapy have regularly described to me their increasing freedom from the rigid and circumscribed life they were leading, while admitting to continuing vulnerability to their original ways of perceiving themselves and others. Other clients say they are content just to be free of crippling anxiety, depression, grief or resentment and able to return to their role in life. Still other clients seek insight and understanding but seem to have reasonably happily decided to continue their lives with more acceptance and understanding of their choices. I notice that these more contented clients have always used therapy for their present stage of personal growth and not for some hypothetical therapeutically correct outcome.

All this leads me to re-affirm the humility needed to be a psychotherapist, who is after all, as Gabrielle indicates above, only present for a miniscule proportion of time in relation to a client's whole life, even when they meet regularly for five hours a week, as in some psychoanalytic practice. There seems to be a strong temptation for us as therapists to view our work with a client as central, and our role as catalyst as major. This view of the therapist as central was evident in the early outcome studies described in Chapter 4 and, in my view, is still implied in the current somewhat obsessive preoccupation of researchers with finding the correct therapy for each particular syndrome of psychological distress, in a search for 'what works for whom?' (Roth and Fonagy 1996). Measurement of outcome is complicated by an array of complex factors including external life changes, improved or deteriorating health and the difficulty in deciding who decides, defines and specifies the outcomes.

No change outcomes

Gabrielle
There have been occasions where I have thought there was no change and the client agreed; but on other occasions there has been a difference in opinion. If both parties agree there has been no change then an ending must be right. But is this judgement too simplistic? Why would my client and I both choose to see no change when I believe that any interaction between two people in which one person is attending and actively listening to the other for at least an hour will affect both people? One answer is that both the client and I are looking for big differences rather than subtle changes arising from remembered interventions and narratives occurring in therapy sessions. It is also possible that the resultant disappointment, arising from the expectation that big changes would occur, masks a realistic appraisal of the actual changes. It is as easy for a therapist as for a client to have high expectations.

It is these high expectations and desire for grandiosity on the therapist's part that probably contribute to the therapist observing no change where the client does experience change – unless it is that the client tells the therapist there is change when there is none. If therapists are using therapy to boost their own ego they may need to see massive rather than subtle change; and clients who sense this may compliantly convey the impression of having produced this level of change.

The idea that subtle changes always take place in any meaningful human interaction may be true, but this may not be satisfactory for some clients. They usually seek therapy because they are very unhappy, perhaps they have no close relationships, or their marriage is in disarray, or they are acutely anxious or stressed. If these situations they are unhappy about do not alter then there is for them no change. If either the therapist feels there is no change or the client says there is no change then it is very important to address this. Is therapy not harnessing the client's motivation? Or is motivation lacking because, for example, the client is seeking therapy to please someone else? If the client's motivation is not harnessed and there is little or no collaboration, then supervision might help a therapist think about what is causing the block or how they might work differently.

Sometimes therapy goes round and round in repetitive circles despite many and varied interventions, and no change happens. When this occurs it might be right to end therapy, with or without referral to another therapist, although the suggestion of closure can in itself unblock an impasse. Another reason for no change is antipathy between a client and therapist. I remember agreeing to work with someone I did not like. The work was blocked until I asked myself why I had such negative feelings about this person and why I had agreed to work with him. On wondering whether he might be used to being disliked, and putting this into words, the therapy started moving, probably because my realization that he expected to be disliked made sense to him.

No change may be the result of the chemistry that exists between two people, mentioned earlier, of not being compatible. There may not be such a strong feeling as 'dislike' or 'hate', but just one of 'not feeling right'. Clients may feel so desperate to find a therapist that they agree to work with someone with whom they are uncomfortable. This discomfort can block therapy. I try to get potential clients to be honest with themselves in the initial assessment and to understand that I will not be offended if they do not feel they can open up to me. This is another occasion where to let someone start a therapeutic relationship with feelings that I know could block therapy is irresponsible.

It may be hard for a therapist to admit that they are unable to help a client and it may be disappointing to both the therapist and the client that change has not taken place. The disappointment can stop both therapist and client from thinking about the need to end. Therapists need the humility to recognize that they may well have played a part in the block, to face that they need to be open about this, and so explore with the client whether ending the therapy is the right course of action. Such exploration does not necessarily result in an ending, but if it does then this must be in the best interests of the client.

Writing about 'no change' seems to produce endless conundrums for me, perhaps because it is not what I want but what the client wants that matters. For clients 'no change' could be a negative or positive outcome and so it wouldn't belong to a separate category. Only the client can be the judge of that. For instance, I have seen several young people who sought therapy because they thought that 'something was wrong with them'. A very brief therapy, often only one or two sessions, convinced them that change was not necessary. In these instances 'no change' was a positive outcome. On other occasions, some of which I describe above, 'no change' was a profoundly disappointing outcome and therefore negative.

Jenifer
I appreciate and share Gabrielle's struggle with the concept of 'no change'. I share in my own practice her rigorous demand for therapy to be in movement rather than blocked. However, I wonder about other therapists and clients who seem less concerned about change and are seemingly content to continue with the process of regular meetings in which the client is listened to by the therapist and the therapist theorizes in their own head about what is going on, and nothing shifts. There is the evidence from the *Consumer Reports* (1995) study commented upon by Seligman (1995) that 'the longer people stay in therapy, the more they improve'. Maybe the experience of being attended to for a considerable length of time is enough for some clients and acceptable to some therapists.

I am less sure about Gabrielle's 'chemistry' argument, that sometimes the 'chemistry' is wrong and so the therapy is blocked. It seems to me that, as with the examples she gives in the previous paragraph, working through uncomfortable feelings and understanding them may reveal some projection from past experience or may be key to the client's ability to tolerate uncomfortable situations. For myself, an attempt to see the client as the child they once were can resolve and dissolve feelings of discomfort, or even strong dislike. Understanding how the client has evolved their way of being in the world usually replaces my feelings of discomfort and/or aversion with them.

As for over-high expectations on the part of either the therapist or the client contributing to a perception of no change, when in fact subtle changes may be taking place, I wonder how this sits with the importance of positive motivation as contributory to outcome (Frank and Frank 1991). Do clients need to have high expectations to engage in therapy and are they right to feel disappointment when nothing seems to be happening? Are therapists who expect little change to happen heading for burn-out? There is a fine line between over-enthusiasm and false hopes. I am left wondering about change again. As already mentioned, if a positive outcome of psychotherapy is to have a broader outlook on life and more options for facing difficulties, then clients are likely to have a 'no change' outcome in many ways.

The effect on outcomes of society, culture and politics

Every human endeavour is influenced by the society, culture and political environment in which it is accomplished. This is as true for the different theoretical models that have evolved as it is for which model is chosen by a particular therapist and then imposed upon the client. Even the outcomes of therapy desired by therapist and client are likely to link back to the culture, society, family of origin and political system in which they have grown up and/or now live. Currently Western society, with its focus on the ideal of individualism and its encouragement to expect gratification, results in clients seeking outcomes that would be unthinkable in the more community based societies of the East. For example a desired outcome to be more autonomous, which has been a dominant ethic in Western based therapies, might be unthinkable where the family or community group is paramount.

If the number of people from ethnic minorities seeking therapy or training as therapists is an indicator, the therapies that have become dominant in Britain are probably not sufficiently multicultural in their approach, despite their efforts to be so. We both know training courses where the trainees from the ethnic minorities have struggled to pass. This may be because issues such as difference, isolation, membership of the in-group, being on the edge and individualism versus community are not sufficiently recognized and valued. In addition the role of therapist in some of the more communally based cultures carries with it an expectation of wisdom and advice giving which is not seen as part of Western therapies with their focus on autonomy. Similar problems arise when members of the ethnic minority are seeking therapy. They can feel very dissatisfied when their desired outcome was to receive instruction on what to do and the therapist seems to be avoiding doing just that.

Psychological therapies evolved in Europe and the US at a time when the power of Christianity was declining (Halmos 1978) and people were able to question what had been seen as the absolute authority of the church. At the same time British society was becoming less deferential to the authority of educated people and the nobility. Therapy, which was subversive, challenging the power and paternalism of the medical profession, teachers, land-owners and the church, arose from this both cultural and societal change and promoted it. Increased autonomy has become a desired outcome of some theoretical orientations and originally had a powerful, subversive effect in society. It is possible that in Britain the decreasing deference to the authority of bodies such as the Church, the medical profession and the educational profession is in part a result of the therapy movement.

Some other theoretical orientations look for increased realism as a desirable outcome of therapy. It may be that society has responded to this drive to increase autonomy and realism in the individual. It is now common for therapists to be summoned whenever a disaster occurs. In one respect this could be seen as an affirmation of the effectiveness of therapy, but it might also be viewed as a way of achieving a particular contemporary outcome, which is that no one should feel dissatisfied in this 'well functioning' society. The presence of therapists remedies a situation and salves any guilt behind any mistakes that have led to a disaster; but at the same time the realism of being human, in a world where mistakes and natural disasters happen, can be covered up and denied, and autonomy countered with this myth that everyone should be happy.

The politically driven need for accountability can have a significant effect on psychotherapeutic outcomes. A positive effect has been the development of brief therapies and the assumption that people will use therapy several times during their lives as the need arises. This changes the objectives and outcomes to smaller but still significant goals. For example, brief therapy for someone who cannot manage at work because of a bereavement might focus on the feelings associated with the loss, normalizing them and explaining the grief reaction. It would not necessarily embark on an exploration of the history of that person's attachments and losses. The objective of brief therapy is to help the client manage the grief and thus be able to return to work. It is not to achieve a more global outcome of understanding themselves and their life history, so that when further losses occur they can grieve without necessarily being unable to work. But one negative effect of the need for accountability and the drive for the quick fix is that where there is genuine need for in-depth and long-term work for someone who has had a major breakdown and mental illness, it is not available at low cost or free at the point of delivery.

Cognitive behavioural therapy is particularly suited to the political agenda of valuing science based beliefs and quantitative evidence based research and rapid outcomes. The practice of CBT has clearly specified outcomes, techniques that can easily be standardized, and aims for an economy of energy and resources. The result is that CBT often comes out as the most effective therapy in evidence based research and thus has become the treatment of choice for many conditions in the NHS. In our experience clients often come to us having found CBT unsatisfactory, too mechanical and superficial. There needs to be some qualitative research looking at clients' experience of CBT, as opposed to humanistic therapies or psychoanalytically based therapies, to see whether CBT really should be the preferred therapy. There is, in any case, an increasing body of opinion that the methodology of evidence based research and its underlying concepts are not fully appropriate to the subtle exploration of psychotherapy outcome (Seligman 1995; Marzillier 2004).

It seems then that society, culture and politics are all likely to influence what goes on in the consulting room. Current societal values and dominant cultural beliefs may be the explicit content of psychotherapy, because clients are likely to present when they feel out of tune with what they perceive as acceptable normal thoughts, feelings and behaviour. This can lead to a positive outcome when a client's sense of dissonance is honestly and fearlessly engaged with so that the client is free to move to a more authentic expression of their own values and beliefs. A more sinister influence is present when these influences are not acknowledged or are covertly accepted as ideal or normal. Then psychotherapy can itself become a political instrument, encouraging, or even enforcing, conformity to accepted societal and cultural norms. The anti-psychiatry criticisms of Laing (1960) and Szasz (1962, 1974) spring to mind, as do Alice Miller's (1987) accusations regarding the 'poisonous pedagogy' practised by many psychoanalysts. What is a positive outcome for the client's family, social group or culture may be a negative outcome for the client, preventing change in the form of expanded options.

What is the purpose of psychotherapy and does it work anyway?

As we conclude our dialogue both of us have become aware of general themes and questions that keep coming into view for both of us, and we want to share our responses. The main question is on the purpose of psychotherapy and counselling, and whether it works. In the first chapter, we responded to a series of questions from our own experience as reasonably experienced practitioners:

● What is my objective/aim in working as a therapist?
● Am I making any difference to my clients' lives?
● Do clients meet their own objectives?
● Is being a therapist a worthwhile occupation?
● Why do some therapeutic relationships work well and others fail?
● How valid is the therapist's explanation for failure or success?

As we engaged with the subsequent chapters, we addressed these and other related questions in the light of different theoretical orientations and a variety of contexts. We explored in some depth the complex interface between research and psychotherapeutic practice; and then we focused upon the way in which assessment/intake sessions influence both the aims and intentions of client and therapist and the outcomes that result from the work they do together.

Now we are left with some basic themes regarding the purpose and function of psychological therapy. Has psychotherapy become such a closed shop that it cannot hear the challenge to find ways of working with clients that meet their needs? Does psychotherapy truly serve the client or has it become a servant of current social and cultural ideologies? Do these ideologies of hedonism, consumerism and individual gratification conceal a push towards conformity with the power possessing political authorities? Are therapists so dominated by their own professional conformities and allegiances that they tend to forget clients' objectives and the potential of psychotherapy to encourage a person to expand their awareness and awaken their fuller potential, even if this leads to a subversion of the current needs and beliefs of state, religion and community? Finally, what is the interface between the goals of psychological therapy and the search for meaning and inner transformation?

One of the effects of professionalization is that organizations do become closed shops, and they become self-serving, self-justifying and self-satisfied. They are then not open to challenge from radical thinkers without or even within the organization, and they certainly do not hear any challenge that comes from clients. Without these challenges there is a danger that practice will fossilize and not develop in response to changing needs. Therapists have been slow to respond to the needs of the younger generation who use email and mobile phone texting very extensively. To our knowledge there has been no article in any of the journals on the use of text by clients or therapists, or the positive role of text messages in the therapeutic journey, although we have heard people criticize their use because they cross boundaries. Here the idea of boundaries may be being used defensively to block change rather than responding to the challenge.

The 'boho' generation mentioned in Chapter 3 are also asking for new ways of working. The danger is that they are categorized as an 'oddity' and their needs ignored. Actually they belong to a group of influential and powerful trendsetters who should be able to find a therapy which recognizes their desired goals, just as much as the 'worried well' with whom therapists frequently work.

Our doubts and fears regarding the use of psychotherapy to promote some sort of conformity are increasingly expressed in this book and have become particularly prominent in this chapter. When we considered the influence of theoretical orientations and the practitioner's affiliation to a particular school or model of therapy, we realized that the belief systems embedded in each approach inevitably promote a specific view of the 'good life'. Clients can be subtly guided towards an adjustment to the social norms of the therapist and of their original teachers. Even humanistic and existential therapies, originally encouraging self-expression, personal responsibility and a search for individual meaning, have tended towards the imposition of somewhat 'politically correct' forms of expression, while criticizing the 'directiveness' of CBT and the 'limiting' interpretations of psychoanalysis. We have commented on the encouragement of a search for instant gratification, which appears to support the fulfilment of individual needs but which can be used to promote the aims of a global economy and the politicians who serve these masters.

More specifically, as in Chapter 3, we noted the pressure exerted by the context in which therapy is carried out, where the aims and objectives are dominated by certain limitations that are imposed upon the therapist and perhaps the client. So, how are practitioners to avoid these powerful external authorities in their work with and for their clients? The answer might be by combining honest recognition of their own bias with constant vigilance about their own unconscious agenda, bringing them both into awareness wherever possible and, very simply but importantly, listening to their clients' own agenda, which might also be hidden. The history of psychoanalysis, psychotherapy and counselling is full of disagreements, leading to ejections from theoretical groups because of a refusal to conform, and subsequent creation of new theories. Frequently there is no acknowledgement of how a 'new' theory has evolved from an existing one, or realization that a similar or overlapping theory already exists within another theoretical orientation. A recent example is the development of 'relational' psychoanalysis (Mitchell and Aaron 1999), which seems to ignore the main thrust of Rogers' work.

We have both heard theories being presented with little mention of clients' objectives, yet there would be no therapists without clients. If theory had developed from the clients' point of view rather than from a focus on theoretical ideas, would there be much more integration and less argument? The argument for 'common factors', which is integrative, arises from the focus being on what clients' need rather than what therapists think they need (Goldfried 1980; Frank and Frank 1991; Bohart and Tallman 1999). A major common factor is the level of motivation and readiness for stage-appropriate therapeutic work. The therapist's work is to engage the client through the relationship, offer a helpful explanation and a way forward which matches the client's experience and current need, and then encourage active experimentation in the client's own external world. Most theoretical orientations could be adapted to these purposes.

Once a theoretical group has formed then conformity is often demanded to maintain the strength of the group against attack. Again this can result in losing sight of clients' objectives and of the potential of therapy to open up unknown worlds and unknown parts of the client so that they can reach towards their full potential. This opening often leads clients to feel able to challenge the orthodoxies of the political, cultural, religious and social systems in which they live and to even challenge the shibboleths of the therapy profession. This potential of therapy is one of the most exciting and rewarding aspects of the work, but is frequently not experienced because of the constrictions put in place by society, and accepted by the theoretical group, when it prizes short-term gains above long-term aspirations.

Psychotherapy has an uneasy relationship with the aspirations of spiritual search. Some established religions have adopted psychological counselling as an extension of spiritual direction. These counselling services are often suspected of having a hidden aim to convert and proselytize their clients and of making their own moral ideals central, so, for example, not being open to a client's need to express feelings of rage and revenge. Many of the professional bodies regulating the provision of psychological therapy are sceptical about any belief that cannot be empirically supported, suggesting that it might be merely a psychological crutch. As a result, many therapies focus on alleviation of present distress and some re-shaping of the client's ways of thinking, feeling and behaving. Other therapies promote some form of transformation whether this is described as self-actualization or getting in touch with a 'higher self'. Rowan (1993) suggests that there are a succession of higher levels of psychotherapy provision that aspire to the development of a client's soul and spirit. Transpersonal psychologies provide methodologies aimed towards these ends. However, there is little discussion of the conflict between the search for a happier and more comfortable self-image and the hard inner work needed to transcend the needs of a tyrannous ego. The more esoteric branches of all the main religions describe this struggle and can be critical of the focus upon replacing rigid and neurotic character traits with a more contented, expanded and integrated personality. Our view is that psychological therapy can prepare the way for the work needed to let go of the individual self-image and to embark on a journey, which is a search for higher levels of consciousness through increased awareness.

As we conclude, we think of three things: the journey we have made together in writing this book, the journey of the reader and the journey of clients. In each case we start out not knowing our actual destination, even if we think we know where we are going. As writers, readers or clients, we cannot begin this journey unless we are ready: readiness is all. Our clients cannot make the journey without courage. And we believe that therapists also have to have courage because birth and death are integral to all we do. At every step we do not know whether it is birth or death we are witnessing or both.

Further reading

Bohart, A.C. and Tallman, K. (1999) *How Clients Make Therapy Work: The Process of Active Self-Healing*. Washington, DC: American Psychological Association.

Frank, J.D. and Frank, J.B. (1991) *Persuasion and Healing: A Comparative Study of Psychotherapy*. London: Johns Hopkins Press.

Leuzinger-Bohleber, M. and Target, M. (2002) *Outcomes of Psychoanalytic Treatment: Perspectives for Therapists and Researchers*. London: Whurr.

McLeod, John (1999) *Practitioner Research in Counselling*. London: Sage.

Roth, A. and Fonagy, P. (2005) *What Works for Whom? A Critical Review of Psychotherapy Research*, 2nd edn. New York: Guilford Press.

Rowland, N. and Goss, S. (2000) *Evidence-Based Counselling and Psychological Therapies: Research and Applications*. London: Routledge.

Seligman, M.E.P. (1995) The effectiveness of psychotherapy: The Consumer Reports study, *American Psychologist*, 50: 965–74. Available at www.apa.org/journals/amp/

Wampold, B. (2001) *The Great Psychotherapy Debate: Models, Methods and Findings*. New Jersey: Lawrence Erlbaum Associate.

References

Alexander, F. and French, T.M. (1946) *Psychoanalytic Therapy: Principles and Applications*. New York: Ronald Press.

American Psychiatric Association (1994) *Diagnostic and Statistical Manual of Mental Disorders*, 4th edn. Washington, DC: American Psychiatric Association.

Barkham, M. and Mellor-Clark, J. (2000) Rigour and relevance: The role of practice-based evidence in the psychological therapies, in N. Rowland and S. Goss (eds) *Evidence-Based Counselling and Psychological Therapies*. London: Routledge.

Barkham, M. and Shapiro, D.A. (1989) Towards resolving the problem of waiting lists: psychotherapy in two-plus-one sessions, *Clinical Psychology Forum*, October, 23: 15–19.

Beck, A.T. (1972) *Depression Causes and Treatment*. Philadelphia: University of Philadelphia Press.

Beck, A.T. (1976) *Cognitive Therapy and the Emotional Disorders*. New York: Penguin Books.

Beck, A.T. (1985) Cognitive Therapy, in J.K. Zeig (ed.) *The Evolution of Psychotherapy*. New York: Brunner/Mazel.

Beck, A.T., Freeman, A. and Associates (1990) *Cognitive Therapy of Personality Disorders*. New York: Guilford Press.

Bergin, A.E. and Lambert, M.J. (1978) The evaluation of psychotherapy outcomes, in S.L. Garfield and A.E. Bergin (eds) *Handbook of Psychotherapy and Behavior Change*. New York: Wiley.

Bohart, A.C. (2000) The client is the most important common factor: Clients' self-healing capacities and psychotherapy, *Journal of Psychotherapy Integration*, 10(2): 128–49.

Bohart, A.C. and Tallman, K. (1999) *How Clients Make Therapy Work: The Process of Active Self-Healing*. Washington, DC: American Psychological Association.

Breuer, J. and Freud, S. ([1895] 1974) *Studies on Hysteria*. Penguin Freud Library, Volume 3. Harmondsworth: Penguin Books.

Buckley, P. (1986) *Essential Papers on Object Relations*. New York: New York University Press.

Butler, G. (1999) *Overcoming Social Anxiety*. Oxford: Warneford Hospital.

Carroll, M. (1996) *Counselling Supervision: Theory, Skills and Practice*. London: Cassell.

Casement, P.J. (1985) *On Learning from the Patient*. London: Tavistock.

Consumer Reports, (1995) Mental health: Does therapy help? November: 734–9.

Cooper, C. (2002) Psychodynamic therapy: the Kleinian approach, in W. Dryden (ed.) *Handbook of Individual Therapy*. London: Sage.

Corey, G. (1986) *Theory and Practice of Counselling and Psychotherapy*. Pacific Grove, CA: Brooks Cole.

Davies, D. and Bhugra, D. (2004) *Models of Psychopathology*. Buckingham: Open University Press.

Dryden, W. (1991) *A Dialogue with John Norcross*. Milton Keynes: Open University Press.

Elliott, R. (1983) 'That in your hands ...' A comprehensive process analysis of a significant event in psychotherapy, *Psychiatry*, 46: 113–27.

Elliott, R. and Shapiro, D.A. (1992) Client and therapist as analysts of significant events, in S.G. Toukmanian and D.L. Rennie (eds) *Psychotherapy Process Research: Paradigmatic and Narrative Approaches*. London: Sage.

Ellis, A. (1962). *Reason and Emotion in Psychotherapy*. Secaucus, NJ: Citadel.

Ellis, A. (1987) The evolution of rational-emotive therapy (RET) and cognitive behavior therapy (CBT), in J.K. Zeig (ed.) *The Evolution of Psychotherapy*. New York: Brunner/Mazel.

Ellis, A. (1994) *Reason and Emotion in Psychotherapy*. New York: Birch Lane Press.

Ellis, M. and Leary-Joyce, J. (2000) Gestalt therapy, in C. Feltham and I. Horton (eds) *Handbook of Counselling and Psychotherapy*. London: Sage.

Elton Wilson, J. (1993) Towards a personal model of councelling. In Dryden, W. (ed) *Questions and Answers in Councelling in Action*. London: Sage.

Elton Wilson, J. (1994) Counselling students, training counsellors: quality within quantity, *British Journal of Guidance and Counselling*, 22(3): 429–55.

Elton Wilson, J. (1996) *Time-Conscious Psychological Therapy: A Life Stage to Go Through*. London: Routledge.

Elton Wilson, J. (2000a) A Professional Doctorate for Psychotherapists, Unpublished doctoral project. London: Middlesex University and Metanoia Institute.

Elton-Wilson, J. (2000b) Integration and eclecticism in brief/time-focused therapy, in S. Palmer and R. Woolfe (eds) *Integrative and Eclectic Counselling and Psychotherapy*. London: Sage.

Elton Wilson, J. and Barkham, M. (1993) A practitioner-scientist approach to psychotherapy process and outcome research, in P. Clarkson and M. Pokorney (eds) *A Handbook of Psychotherapy*. London: Routledge.

Eysenck, H.J. (1952) The effects of psychotherapy: an evaluation, *Journal of Consulting Psychology*, 16: 319–24.

Eysenck, H.J. (1966) *The Effects of Psychotherapy*. New York: International Science Press.

Feltham, C. and Horton, I. (eds) (2000) *Handbook of Counselling and Psychotherapy*. London: Sage.

Fergusson, L. (2004) Through anxiety and agoraphobia – my story, in T. Simpson (ed.) *Doorways in the Night*. London: Local Voices Publication.

Foskett, J. and Jacobs, M. (1989) Pastoral counselling, in W. Dryden, D. Charles-Edwards and R. Woolfe (eds) *Handbook of Counselling in Britain*. London: Routledge.

France, A. (1988) *Consuming Psychotherapy*. London: Free Association Books.

Frank, J.D. and Frank, J.B. (1991) *Persuasion and Healing: A Comparative Study Of Psychotherapy*. London: Johns Hopkins Press.

Freud, S. ([1920] 1984) *Beyond the Pleasure Principle*. Penguin Freud Library, Volume 11. Harmondsworth: Penguin Books.

Freud, S. (1926) *Inhibitions, Symptoms and Anxiety*, Standard Edition 20. London: Hogarth Press.

Freud, S. ([1933] 1973) *New Introductory Lectures on Psychoanalysis*. Penguin Freud Library, Volume 2. Harmondsworth: Penguin Books.

Garrett, T. (1994) Sexual contact between psychotherapists and their patients, in P. Clarkson and M. Pokorny (eds) *The Handbook of Psychotherapy*. London: Routledge.

George, C., Kaplan, N. and Main, M. (1985) Adult Attachment Interview Protocol, Unpublished manuscript. Berkeley, CA: University of California at Berkeley.

Gerhardt, S. (2004) *Why Love Matters*. London: Brunner-Routledge.

Goldfried, M.R. (1980) Towards the delineation of therapeutic change principles, *American Psychologist*, 35: 991–9.

Goldfried, M.R. (2003) Keynote speech at Metanoia Institute conference, London.

Goldfried, M.R. and Wolfe, B.E. (1996) Psychotherapy practice and research: repairing a strained alliance, *American Psychologist*, 35:1007–16.

Goulding, M. and Goulding, R. (1979) *Changing Lives Through Redecision Therapy*. New York: Brunner/Mazel.

Greenberg, E. (1998) *A Brief Guide to Borderline, Narcissistic and Schizoid Disorders*. New York: Author printed handout.

Greenberger, D. and Padesky, C. (1995) *Mind over Mood*. London: Guilford Press.

Grencavage, L.M. and Norcross, J.C. (1990) Where are the commonalities among the therapeutic common factors? *Professional Psychology: Research and Practice*, 21: 374–6.

Grissom, R.J. (1996) The magical number .7 + .2: Meta-meta-analysis of the probability of superior outcome in comparisons involving therapy, placebo and control, *Journal of Consulting and Clinical Psychology*, 64: 973–82.

Halmos, P. (1978) *The Faith of Counsellors*. London: Constable.

Hanson, J.E. (2004) Should your lips be zipped? How therapist self-disclosure and non-disclosure affects clients, *Counselling and Psychotherapy Research*, 4(1): 37.

Hazler, R.J. (2001) Core conditions of the cognitive-behavioural environment, in R.J. Hazler and N. Barwick (eds) *The Therapeutic Environment*. Buckingham: Open University Press.

Holmes, J. (1995) How I assess for psychoanalytic psychotherapy, in C. Mace (ed.) *The Art and Science of Assessment in Psychotherapy*. London: Routledge.

Horton, I. (2000) Models of counselling and psychotherapy, in C. Feltham and I. Horton (eds) *Handbook of Counselling and Psychotherapy*. London: Sage.

Hovland, C.V. and Rosenberg, M.J. (eds) (1960) *Attitude Organisation and Change*. Haven: Yale.

Howard, K.I., Kopta, S.M., Krause, M.S. and Orlinsky, D.E. (1986) The dose-effect relationship in psychotherapy, *American Psychologist*, 41: 159–64.

Howarth, I. (1988). Psychotherapy: who benefits? *The Psychologist*, 2: 150–2.

Jacobs, M. (1988) *Psychodynamic Counselling in Action*. London: Sage.

Janov, A. (1970) *The Primal Scream: The Cure of Neurosis*. New York: Putnam.

Jung, C.G. ([1954] 1966) *The Collected Works of C.G. Jung, Volume 16: The Practice of Psychotherapy*. London: Routledge & Kegan Paul.

Kagan, N. (1980) Influencing human interaction: 18 years with IPR, in A.K. Hess (ed.) *Psychotherapy Supervision: Theory, Research and Practice*. Chichester: Wiley.

Kelly, G. ([1955] 1991) *The Psychology of Personal Constructs, Volumes I and II*. London: Routledge.

Kovel, J. (1976) *A Complete Guide to Therapy*. New York: Pantheon.

Laing, R.D. (1960) *The Divided Self: An Existential Study in Sanity and Madness*. London: Tavistock.

Lambert, M.J., Shapiro, D.A. and Bergin, A.E. (1986) The effectiveness of psychotherapy, in S.L. Garfield and A.E. Bergin (eds) *Handbook of Psychotherapy and Behavior Change*, 3rd edn. New York: John Wiley and Sons.

Lapworth, P., Sills, C. and Fish, S. (2001) *Integration in Counselling and Psychotherapy*. London: Sage.

Lazarus, A.A. (1981) *The Practice of Multi-Modal Therapy*. New York: McGraw-Hill.

Lazarus, A.A. (1985) *Casebook of Multi-Modal Therapy*. New York: Guilford Press.

Leuzinger-Bohleber, M. and Target, M. (2002) *Outcomes of Psychoanalytic Treatment: Perspectives for Therapists and Researchers*. London: Whurr.

Linehan, M. (1993) *Skills Training Manual for Treating Borderline Personality Disorder*. New York: Guilford Press.

Linehan, M. (1995) *Cognitive-Behavioral Treatment of Borderline Personality Disorder*. New York: Guilford Press.

Luborsky, L., Singer, B. and Luborsky, L. (1975) Comparative studies of psychotherapies: is it true that 'Everyone has won and all must have prizes'?, *Archives of General Psychiatry*, 32: 995–1008.

Mace, C. (1995) When are questionnaires helpful?, in C. Mace (ed.) *The Art and Science of Assessment in Psychotherapy*. London: Routledge.

Mackewn, J. (1997) *Developing Gestalt Counselling*. London: Sage

Malan, D.H. (1975) *A Study of Brief Psychotherapy*. New York: Plenum/Rosetta.

Mann, J. (1973) *Time Limited Psychotherapy*. Cambridge MA: Harvard University Press.

Marzillier, J. (2004) The myth of evidence-based psychotherapy, *The Psychologist*, 17(7): 392–5.

Masterson, J.F. (1985) *The Real Self: A Developmental, Self and Object Relations Approach.* New York: Brunner/Mazel.

McLeod, J. (1994) *Doing Counselling Research.* London: Sage.

McLeod, J. (1999) *Practitioner Research in Counselling.* London: Sage.

McLeod, J. (2000) Narrative therapy, in C. Feltham and I. Horton (eds) *Handbook of Counselling and Psychotherapy.* London: Sage.

McLeod, J. (2001) Developing a research tradition consistent with the practices and values of counselling and psychotherapy: why counselling and psychotherapy research is necessary, *Counselling and Psychotherapy Research,* 1(1): 3–11.

Mearns, D. and Cooper, M. (2005) *Working at Relational Depth in Counselling and Psychotherapy.* London: Sage.

Mellor-Clark, J. (2000) *Counselling in Primary Care in the Context of the NHS Quality Agenda: The Facts.* Rugby: BACP.

Mellor-Clark, J. and Barkham, M. (1997) Evaluating effectiveness: needs, problems and potential benefits, in I. Horton and V. Varma (eds) *The Needs of Counsellors and Psychotherapists.* London: Sage.

Miller, A. (1987) *The Drama of Being a Child.* London: Virago Press.

Mitchell, S.A. and Aaron, I. (eds) (1999) *Relational Psychoanalysis. The Emergence of a Tradition.* Hillsdale, NJ: Analytic Press.

Morrow-Bradley, C. and Elliott, R. (1986) Utilization of psychotherapy research by practicing psychotherapists, *American Psychologist,* 41(2): 188–97.

Moustakis, C. (1994) *Phenomenological Research Methods.* London: Sage.

Peake, T.H., Borduin, C.M. and Archer, R.P. (1988) *Brief Psychotherapies: Changing Frames of Mind.* London: Sage.

Perls, F.S., Hefferline, R.F. and Goodman, P. (1951) *Gestalt Therapy: Excitement and Growth in Human Personality.* New York: Julian Press.

Pilgrim, D. (1993) *A Sociology of Mental Health and Illness.* Buckingham: Open University Press.

Pilgrim, D. (1997) *Psychotherapy and Society.* London: Sage.

Prochaska, J.O. and DiClemente, C.C. (1986) The transtheoretical approach, in J.C. Norcross (ed.) *Handbook of Eclectic Psychotherapy.* New York: Brunner/Mazel.

Rachman, S.J. (1977) Double standards and single standards, *Bulletin of the British Psychological Society,* 30: 295.

Rachman, S.J. and Wilson, G.T. (1980) *The Effects of Psychological Therapy.* New York: Wiley.

Reich, W. (1942) *The Function of Orgasm.* New York: Orgone Institute Press.

Reich, W. (1949) *Character Analysis*. New York: Orgone Institute Press.

Rennie, D.L. (1990) Toward a representation of the client's experience of the psychotherapy hour, in G. Lietaer, J. Rombauts and R. Van Balen (eds) *Client Centered and Experiential Therapy in the Nineties*. Leuven: University of Leuven Press.

Rogers, C.R. (1957) The necessary and sufficient conditions of therapeutic personality change, *Journal of Counselling Psychology*, 21(2): 15–17.

Rogers, C.R. (1967) *On Becoming a Person: A Therapist's View of Psychotherapy*. London: Constable.

Rosenzweig, S. (1936) Some implicit common factors in diverse methods of psychotherapy: 'At last the Dodo said, "Everybody has won and all must have prizes"', *American Journal of Orthopsychiatry*, 6: 412–15.

Roth, A. and Fonagy, P. (1996) *What Works for Whom? A Critical Review of Psychotherapy Research*. New York: Guilford Press.

Roth, A.D. and Parry, G. (1998) The implications of psychotherapy research for clinical practice and service development: lessons and limitations, *Psychotherapy Section Newsletter*, 23: 30–48.

Rowan, J. (1993) *The Transpersonal, Psychotherapy and Counselling*. London: Routledge.

Rowland, N. and Goss, S. (eds) (2000) *Evidence-Based Counselling and Psychological Therapies*. London: Routledge.

Ryle, A. (1990) *Cognitive-Analytic Therapy: Active Participation in Change*. Chichester: Wiley.

Schore, A.N. (1994) *Affect Regulation and the Origin Of Self: The Neurobiology of Emotional Development*. Mahwah, NJ: Erlbaum.

Schore, A.N. (2001) Minds in the making: attachment, the self-organising brain, and developmentally-oriented psychoanalytic psychotherapy, *British Journal of Psychotherapy*, 17, 299–328.

Schore, A.N. (2003) *Affect Regulation and the Repair of Self*. New York: Norton.

Seligman, M.E.P. (1995) The effectiveness of psychotherapy: the consumer reports study, *American Psychologist*, 50: 965–74.

SEPI (Society for the Exploration of Psychotherapy Integration) Amsterdam (2004) 'The Impossible Enterprise? An examination of the Effective Use of Objectives and Outcomes in the Practice of Psychological Therapy', *XX Annual Meeting Programme*. Amsterdam: SEPI.

Shapiro, D.A. and Shapiro, D. (1982) Meta-analysis of comparative therapy outcome studies: a replication and refinement, *Psychological Bulletin*, 92: 581–604.

Shostrom, E. (ed.) (1965) *Three Approaches to Psychotherapy: Client-Centered Therapy*. Film production. Orange, CA: Psychological Films.

Sifneos, P.E. (1979) *Short-term Dynamic Psychotherapy: Evaluation and Technique*. New York: Plenum Medical Book Company.

Sills, C. (1997) *Contracts in Counselling*. London: Sage.

Smith, M.L. and Glass, G.V. (1977) Meta-analysis of psychotherapy outcome studies, *American Psychologist*, 32: 752–60.

Smith, M.L., Glass, G.V. and Miller, T.I. (1980) *The Benefits of Psychotherapy*. Baltimore: The Johns Hopkins University Press.

Sogyal Rinpoche (1992) *The Tibetan Book of Living and Dying*. London: Rider.

Stern, D.N. (1985) *The Interpersonal World of the Infant*. New York: Basic Books.

Stewart, H. (1997) The work of the psychoanalyst, *Institute of Psycho-Analysis News and Events*. London: Institute of Psychoanalyses.

Stewart, I. and Joines, V. (1987) *TA Today: A New Introduction to Transactional Analysis*. Nottingham: Lifespace Publishing.

Strawbridge, S. (2001) Issues relating to the use of psychiatric diagnostic categories in counselling psychology, counselling and psychotherapy: What do you think? in consultation with Pam James, *Counselling Psychology Review*, 16(1): 4–8.

Strenger, C. (2003) *The Designed Self: Psychoanalysis and Contemporary Identities*. London: The Analytic Press.

Syme, G. (1994) *Counselling in Independent Practice*. Buckingham: Open University Press.

Syme, G. (2003) *Dual Relationships in Counselling and Psychotherapy*. London: Sage.

Szasz, T. (1962) *The Myth of Mental Illness*. London: Secker and Warburg.

Szasz, T.S. (1974) *The Myth of Mental Illness*. New York: Harper & Row.

Talmon, M. (1990) *Single Session Therapy*. San Francisco: Jossey Bass.

Tantam, D. (1995) Why assess?, in C. Mace (ed.) *The Art and Science of Assessment in Psychotherapy*. London: Routledge.

Thorne, B. (2002) Person-centred therapy, in W. Dryden (ed.) *Handbook of Individual Therapy*. London: Sage.

Tillich, P. (1952) *The Courage to Be*. New Haven: Yale University Press.

Totton, N. (2003) *Body Psychotherapy*. Maidenhead: Open University Press.

Truax, C.B. and Carkhuff, R.R. (1967) *Towards Effective Counseling and Practice*. Chicago: Aldine.

van Deurzen, E. (2002) Existential therapy, in W. Dryden (ed.) *Handbook of Individual Therapy*. London: Sage.

Wachtel, P.L. (1977) *Psychoanalysis and Behaviour Therapy: Toward an Integration*. New York: Plenum Press.

Wampold, B.E. (2001) *The Great Psychotherapy Debate: Models, Methods and Findings*. New Jersey: Lawrence Erlbaum Associates.

Wampold, B.E., Mondin, G.W., Moody, M. et al. (1997) A meta-analysis of outcome studies comparing bona fide psychotherapies: empirically, 'All must have prizes', *Psychological Bulletin*, 122: 203–15.

Whitmore, D. (2000) Psychosynthesis, in C. Feltham and I. Horton (eds) *Handbook of Counselling and Psychotherapy*. London: Sage.

Winnicott, D.W. ([1954] 1992) The depressive position in normal emotional development, *Through Paediatrics to Psycho-Analysis*. London: Karnac Books.

Winnicott, D.W. (1971) *Playing and Reality*. London: Tavistock Publications.

Wolpe, J. (1982) *The Practice of Behavior Therapy*, 3rd edn. New York: Pergamon Press.

Worth Reading! (2003) (Therapy Book Club Author Events) *Worth Reading! Newsletter*, October: 4.

Yalom, I.D. (1980) *Existential Psychotherapy*. New York: Basic Books.

Yalom, I.D. (2001) *The Gift of Therapy: Reflection on Being a Therapist*. London: Piatkus.

Yalom, I. and Elkin, G. (1974) *Every Day Gets a Little Closer: A Twice-Told Therapy*. New York: Basic Books.

Young, J. and Swift, W. (1988) Schema-focused cognitive therapy for personality disorders, Part I, *International Cognitive Therapy Newsletter*, 4(5): 13–14.

Index